The Information Superhighway: Issues and Challenges

The Information Superhighway: Issues and Challenges

A.P. Cameli (Editor)

Nova Sciences Publishers, Inc.
Commack

Art Director: Maria Ester Hawrys
Assistant Director: Elenor Kallberg
Graphics: Denise Dieterich, Kerri Pfister,
Erika Cassatti and Barbara Minerd
Manuscript Coordinator: Sharyn Schweidel
Book Production: Tammy Sauter, Benjamin Fung
Circulation: Irene Kwartiroff and Annette Hellinger

Library of Congress Cataloging–in–Publication Data available upon request

ISBN 1-56072-304-1

6080 Jericho Turnpike, Suite 207
Commack, New York 11725
Tele. 516-499-3103 Fax 516-499-3146
E Mail Novasci1@aol.com

Printed in the United States of America

Contents

Part A: Issues Affecting Development

Part B: An Overview of Technology Challenges

Preface

The 'information superhighway' is clearly very significant today and in the future of communications. But what is it? One hears about the 'hardware' and the 'software' and about content providers. We are told that we will never have to go outside again to breath fresh air. Everything can be done on the Web or the Net and much better than in person.

One of the messier sets of questions surrounding this issue is who will make the zillions of dollars of profits to finish construction of this modern day Hydra. And who, if anyone, will police it since the evil souls prowling on society are just frothing at the opportunities before them? Will we let our children be vulnerable to the many seductive lures waiting behind a simple mouse click?

The volume combines two GAO reports, GAO/RCED-94-285 and GAO/AIMD-95-23 which we have combined and distilled in an effort to make some sense out of the information superhighway as it nears completion. What flows to us will be determined to a certain extent by the issues discussed in these reports. One hopes that a measure of good will result from this latest incursion into our lives.

A.P. Cameli,
April 1996

PART A
ISSUES AFFECTING DEVELOPMENT

Abbreviations

AIN	advanced intelligent network
ARPA	Advanced Research Projects Agency
AT&T	American Telephone and Telegraph Company
ATM	asynchronous transfer mode
B-ISDN	Broadband Integrated Services Digital Network
BOC	Bell operating company
CAP	competitive access provider
DOD	Department of Defense
FCC	Federal Communications Commission
GEO	geosynchronous Earth orbit
HPCC	High Performance Computing and Communications
Hz	Hertz
IBM	International Business Machines
IDEA	international data encryption algorithm
IITF	Information Infrastructure Task Force
ISDN	Integrated Services Digital Network
Kbps	thousand bits per second
LAN	local area network
LEO	low Earth orbit
Mbps	million bits per second
NANP	North American Numbering Plan
NII	national information infrastructure
NIST	National Institute of Standards and Technology
NSA	National Security Agency
OSI	Office of Special Investigations
PCN	personal communications network
PCS	personal communication system
SAC	service access code
SONET	synchronous optical network
SS7	Signaling System 7
VF	voice frequency
VSAT	very small aperture terminal

Chapter 1

INTRODUCTION

The term "National Information Infrastructure" - commonly known as the "Information Superhighway"[1] - refers collectively to the hardware, software, standards, personnel, and training facilities that will one day form an information infrastructure that will place vast quantities of voice, video and data at users' fingertips. Delivery of these services is being made possible by advances in digital communications, which allow voice, video, and data to travel together over any type of telecommunications medium. These developments are unfolding against a financial and regulatory backdrop that limits the expansion plans of major segments of the telecommunications industry. Recognizing that the regulatory structure of the telecommunications industry needs updating, lawmakers are considering sweeping changes designed to provide a framework that will promote competition and innovation while protecting consumers over the coming decades.

TELECOMMUNICATIONS ENCOMPASSES MANY TECHNOLOGIES

Telecommunications, which we define as voice, video, or data (textual information) transmission, travels over a variety of wired and wireless networks.[2] Telephone networks carry primarily voice conversations over a combination of copper wire and fiber-optic cable, connecting the caller and receiver through a system of switches. Cellular telephone

---

1 The administration has used the terms "National Information Infrastructure" and "Information Superhighway" synonymously.

2 A network is a group of interconnected communications facilities and devices used to transmit information.

networks use a combination of wired and wireless technology to connect the caller with the receiver. Television and radio stations send their signals through the airwaves over broadcast networks, while cable television signals reach the television set through a wired network. Data normally travel between computers over telephone wires. On the horizon are developing technologies that could add networks for satellite television and wireless personal communications services (PCS) that could allow anyone, anywhere, to send and receive voice, video, and data.

THE INFORMATION SUPERHIGHWAY WOULD INTEGRATE TECHNOLOGIES INTO A SEAMLESS WEB

The concept of the Information Superhighway integrates these individual telecommunications networks into a seamless web that would allow information to travel over wires, be transferred to an over-the-air network, and be transferred among networks as it moves from sender to receiver. The administration believes that the Information Superhighway could unleash an "information revolution" that would change forever the way people live, work, and interact with each other. Figure 1.1 illustrates conceptually how the Information

Figure 1.1: Conceptual Illustration of the Information Superhighway

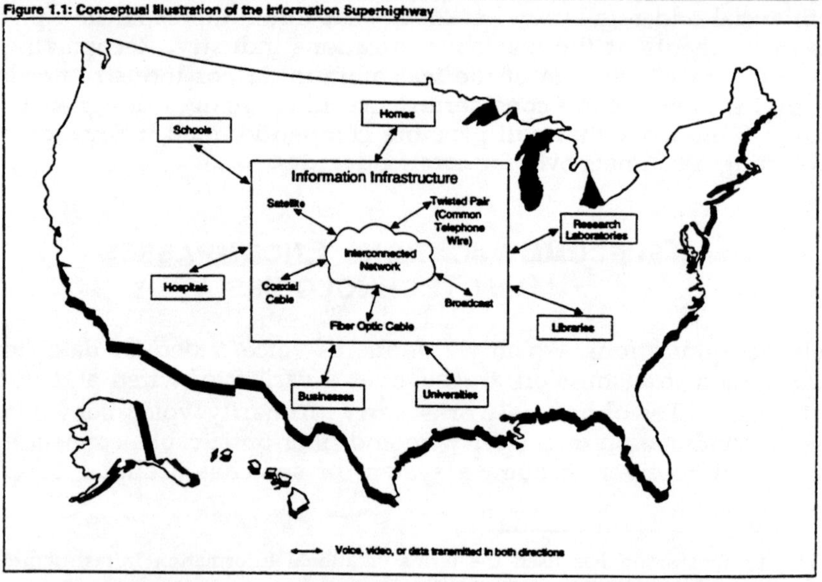

Figure 1.1: Conceptual Illustration of the Information Superhighway

Superhighway might function. The superhighway could, for example, expand opportunities for students in rural or inner-city schools to have access to top-level instructional programming transmitted from distant learning centers. Rural doctors could transmit X-rays or test results to experts at leading medical centers. Businesses could more easily connect with customers and suppliers, improve communications among employees, and gather competitive data. Finally, individuals could enjoy more work/home flexibility by telecommuting - working from home while maintaining contact with the office through telephone, fax, and personal computer.

The Information Superhighway could also affect life in the home. Through interactive television, viewers would no longer be subject to programming schedules. Instead, they could select a previously recorded program - such as a movie, news report, or sporting event - and view it on their televisions. In addition, they could pause, reverse, or fast-forward the program, as they can today in viewing video tapes. Using the Information Superhighway, consumers could electronically select merchandise now available through mail-order catalogs. While many of these services are currently available on a limited scale, all of them could become a routine part of everyday life through the Information Superhighway.

Although no one knows exactly how the superhighway will evolve, the Internet provides current-day examples of the types of services that the Information Superhighway could provide. The Internet began about 25 years ago as a federal effort to investigate computer networking technology under the Advanced Research Projects Agency of the Department of Defense. Today, the Internet connects users to a network of networks that spans all parts of the United States and other sites around the world, and it supports activities in the federal government, universities, and industry research laboratories. The core of the Internet operates over federal "backbone" networks, including those of the National Science Foundation, the National Aeronautics and Space Administration, the Department of Energy, and the Department of Defense. Most users obtain access to the Internet backbone through numerous other networks that, collectively, form the Internet.

Digitization Makes it All Possible

Digitization makes telecommunications signals interchangeable, thus allowing signals from different sources to travel over various types of infrastructure. Digitization translates voice, data, and video signals into the common language of computers - "ones" and "zeros" called "bits." This process greatly increases flexibility in determining whether the signals must be sent over a specific type of infrastructure.

Through digitization, the Information Superhighway can carry any type of "freight" in the form of bits - be they voice, video or data - from the source to the user.

Increases in Infrastructure Capacity are Required

In order to carry interactive video services, some portions of the telecommunications infrastructure require greater capacity. High-capacity "broadband" fiber-optic cable, which could carry many Information Superhighway services, exists in the interstate, long-distance portion of the infrastructure.[3] However, the local infrastructure, largely consisting of copper telephone wire and coaxial cable television wire, has lower capacity. While copper telephone wire enters about 95 percent of U.S. residences and businesses and provides interactive, two-way communications, its low capacity would prevent some Information Superhighway services (e.g., interactive video) from reaching users in many homes, schools, libraries, or medical centers. Coaxial cable, which is used for cable television, is available to about 95 percent, and enters about 60 percent of U.S. residences. It has about 900 times the capacity of copper wire. Although the capacity of coaxial cable is not as great as that of fiber-optic cable, coaxial cable could meet most of the currently envisioned residential requirements for Information Superhighway services. However, to carry interactive two-way traffic, the cable infrastructure's delivery systems must be upgraded. According to an industry trade association, such upgrades would cost about $20 billion.

Existing Legal and Regulatory Structure Sets the Stage for Potential Changes

The Communications Act of 1934 established the Federal Communications Commission (FCC) as an independent agency

> "for the purpose of regulating interstate and foreign commerce in communication by wire and radio so as to make available, so far as possible, to all the people of the United States a rapid, efficient, nationwide and world-wide wire and radio communications service with adequate facilities at reasonable charges."

As enacted, the act focused on telephone and radio, but it was not restricted to any particular technology. The act now covers many new

[3] For additional information on capacity and other aspects of telecommunications technology, see appendix I. This report also contains a glossary of telecommunications terms.

technologies such as cable television, cellular telephones, and satellite communications. The act generally left regulation of intrastate services to the states. Appendix II provides information on the other agencies that establish or influence telecommunications policy and the diverse set of businesses that make up the telecommunications industry.

Following the passage of the Communications Act of 1934, the American Telephone and Telegraph Company (AT&T) continued to operate as a regulated monopoly but generally remained subject to federal antitrust laws. Throughout the 1950s and 1960s competitive pressures mounted from innovations in customer premises equipment (e.g., telephones) and improvements in radio technology. FCC responded with a number of regulatory decisions that allowed limited competition in specific markets. In 1974, the United States issued the third of three major antitrust actions against AT&T, each of which ended in a settlement agreement. The 1974 action was settled in 1982 through a consent decree that was approved with modifications by the court.

The 1982 consent decree significantly changed the regulatory landscape of the telecommunications industry by generally separating the competitive segments of the telephone industry - long-distance service and customer premises equipment - from what was viewed as a natural monopoly[4] - local telephone service. The decree divested AT&T of its 22 local telephone service companies, called Bell operating companies (BOCS).

Today the BOCS, together with GTE, a holding company for 24 local telephone companies, and nearly 1,300 other local telephone companies provide local telephone service.[5] AT&T continues to provide long-distance service in competition with other long-distance carriers. Unlike the days before divestiture when a single company provided a majority of service, long-distance calls now travel over competitive long-distance carriers' lines for the long-distance portion of the call, and through the local telephone company's infrastructure to complete long-distance connections, while FCC regulations imposed similar requirements on other local telephone companies. The local telephone companies charge the long-distance companies access fees to route long-distance calls through the local telephone lines.

---

4 A natural monopoly exists when the costs of production decline as additional output is produced so that a single producer can supply the entire market cheaper than any combination of two or more producers.

5 AT&T's consent decree does not apply to GTE or to other local telephone companies. However, in the early 1980s, the government filed an antitrust action against GTE ghallenging GTE's acquisition of the telecommunication enterprises of Southern Pacific Corp. (which operated Spring long-distance service). Under a court-approved consent decree, the acquisition was permitted subject to a number of conditions, including that GTE's local monopoly operations be kept separate from its long-distance and other competitive operations. In 1993, GTE was the second largest telephone company in terms of revenue and fourth in terms of access lines.

Industry is Converging, Providing Competitive Opportunities

Against this legal and regulatory backdrop, the telecommunications industry is undergoing substantial change. The emerging ability to transmit data, voice, and video through a variety of methods is stimulating formerly separate segments of the industry to diversify product lines and to take advantage of complementary strengths. For example, some large telephone companies see opportunities to compete in their existing service areas with cable and broadcast television companies by transmitting or providing video programming over telephone lines, while cable television companies are considering providing local telephone service over their infrastructure, in competition with the telephone companies.

To optimally position themselves to provide diversified services, these formerly separate segments of the telecommunications industry are considering mergers and strategic alliances. Cable companies believe that the large telephone company's substantial cash flows will help them upgrade their systems to provide telephone service, while the telephone companies believe that the cable companies' experience in managing and marketing video services will be a critical asset to compete successfully in the video programming market. Additionally, the large telephone companies and long-distance companies are acquiring or investing in cellular telephone companies to broaden their networks and take advantage of advances in wireless technology.

Some such mergers have already occurred. Southwestern Bell has purchased a cable system in Montgomery County, Maryland, through which it plans to begin offering local telephone services. Sprint, a long-distance provider, merged with Central Cellular company, which at the time of the merger was the nation's ninth largest cellular provider.

Legislative Changes Have Been Proposed

Lawmakers are considering legislation designed to allow increased competition in the telecommunications industry. The proposed legislation addresses several major issues, such as whether federal legislation should supersede state laws that prohibit local telephone competition; whether and under what conditions the BOCs should be allowed entry into long-distance telephone service; whether and under what conditions local telephone companies, including the BOCs, should be allowed to provide video services in their service areas; how to ensure competitor's equal access to local, long-distance and cellular infrastructures; and how to ensure that no consumers lose access to telecommunications services because of rate increases. In addition, the legislation would shift much of the locus of responsibility for overseeing BOC's entry into certain competitive markets from the courts, where it has resided since 1984, to the executive branch of the federal government.

Decision Makers Face Several Issues

The prospect of a restructured telecommunications industry that would collectively build and operate an Information Superhighway raises a number of issues. Chapter 2 discusses the central issues related to reducing barriers to local telecommunications competition. Chapter 3 discusses the issues associated with providing universal service in a competitive environment, and chapter 4 provides an overview of some of the pressing technical challenges that decision makers will face as the Information Superhighway develops.

Objective, Scope, and Methodology

Under our basic legislative responsibility to prepare evaluations of issues that the Comptroller General believes will assist the Congress, we reviewed issues facing decision makers as they develop new telecommunications laws and regulations to facilitate the development of the Information Superhighway. These issues include (1) managing the transition to a more competitive local telecommunications marketplace; (2) ensuring that all consumers have access to affordable telecommunications as competition develops; and (3) ensuring that the Information Superhighway provides adequate security, privacy, reliability and interoperability.

To determine the central issues facing decision makers, we reviewed an extensive body of reports, white papers, and industry statements. We held discussions with officials at FCC, the Department of Commerce (the National Institute of Standards and Technology and the National Telecommunications and Information Administration), the National Science Foundation, the Department of Education, the Office of Technology Assessment, the Department of Defense, the National Security Agency, and the Rural Electrification Administration. We also met with representatives of a long-distance carrier and of the United States Telephone Association. To keep abreast of legislative developments, we closely followed the numerous congressional hearings on telecommunications issues held during 1993 and 1994. We conducted our work between October 1993 and August 1994.

Chapter 2

REDUCING BARRIERS TO LOCAL COMPETITION MAY HELP BUILD THE INFORMATION SUPERHIGHWAY, BUT PRESENTS CHALLENGES

Technological advances and competition in the long-distance market have led to infrastructure improvements needed to support the interstate portion of the Information Superhighway. However, the local infrastructure needs significant improvement to bring the superhighway to homes, businesses, and schools. Local infrastructure improvements have begun, stimulated in part by the limited competition that has begun to emerge in local telephone services. However, legal and regulatory barriers, established to maintain affordable residential telephone rates and protect consumers from the local telephone company's monopoly power, limit the extent to which competition can develop at the local level. Consequently, the Congress is considering regulatory revisions aimed at removing barriers to transforming the local market from one dominated by the local telephone company to one that is more competitive while retaining appropriate safeguards. However, disagreement exists over whether and to what extent consumers will need protection from the local telephone company's market power.

TECHNOLOGICAL ADVANCES AND COMPETITION LED TO IMPROVEMENTS IN THE LONG-DISTANCE INFRASTRUCTURE

The divestiture of AT&T, which became effective in 1984, helped facilitate the growth of competition in the long-distance telephone service market. Spurred by advances in technology, some competitors had been attempting to establish a competitive foothold in the long-distance market since FCC first authorized competitive entry in 1969. However, at the time of divestiture, AT&T held 92 percent of total long-distance revenues. As figure 2.1 shows, AT&T's market share steadily decreased after 1984 but remained well over 50 percent in 1993.

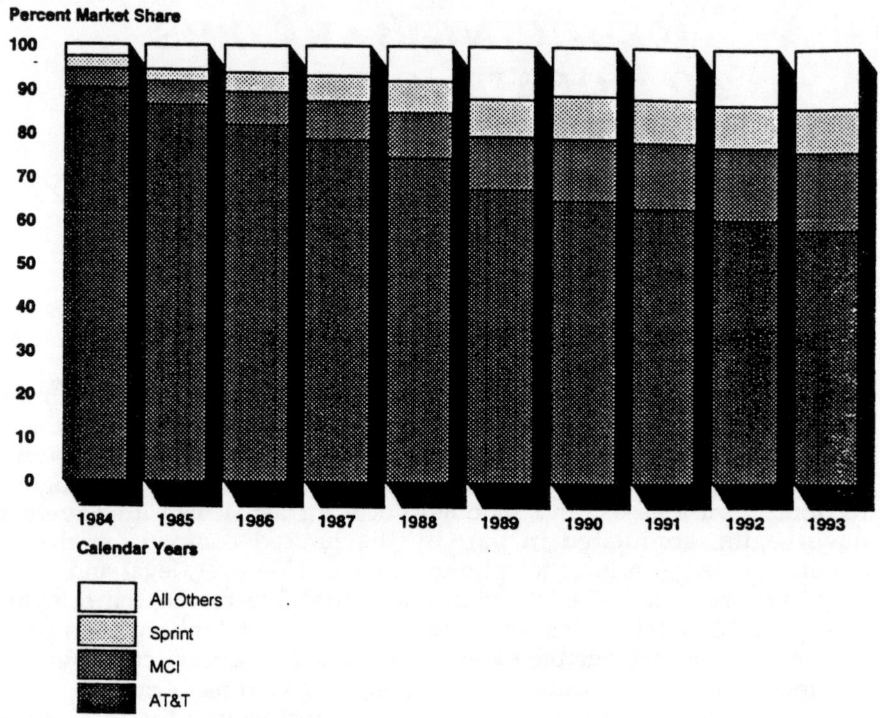

Figure 2.1. Percentage of Long-Distance Revenues of AT&T, MCI, Sprint, and All Other Long-Distance Carriers, 1984-93

The consent decree, together with FCC requirements that local telephone companies provide every long-distance competitor equal access to the local infrastructure, enhanced the ability of new long-distance companies to compete with AT&T. While other long distance providers - MCI, Sprint, and AT&T - hold most of the long-distance market, FCC estimated that about 400 long-distance carriers were in business as of January 1994, allowing customers to choose among a wide range of services, pricing arrangements, and service options. Because of its significant market share, AT&T has remained subject to FCC's regulatory oversight for long-distance services.

Since the divestiture, consumers have benefited from lower prices and the long-distance infrastructure has been significantly upgraded. As figure 2.2 shows, published tariff rates declined sharply between 1984 and 1989 and more slowly since then,[6] while long-distance usage has increased, as figure 2.3 shows.

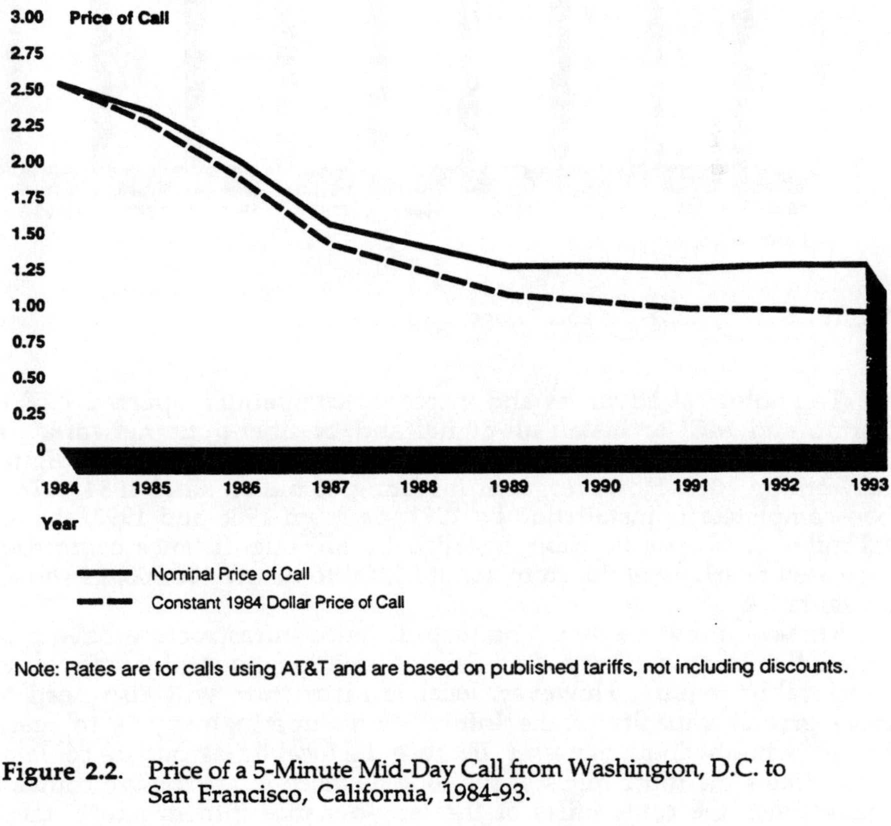

Note: Rates are for calls using AT&T and are based on published tariffs, not including discounts.

Figure 2.2. Price of a 5-Minute Mid-Day Call from Washington, D.C. to San Francisco, California, 1984-93.

---

6 A representative of a long-distance carriers' association noted that tariff rates do not represent what consumers actually pay because the tariffed rates do not reflect the variety of discount plans offered by the industry. The representative said rates actually paid by consumers are lower than tariffed rates.

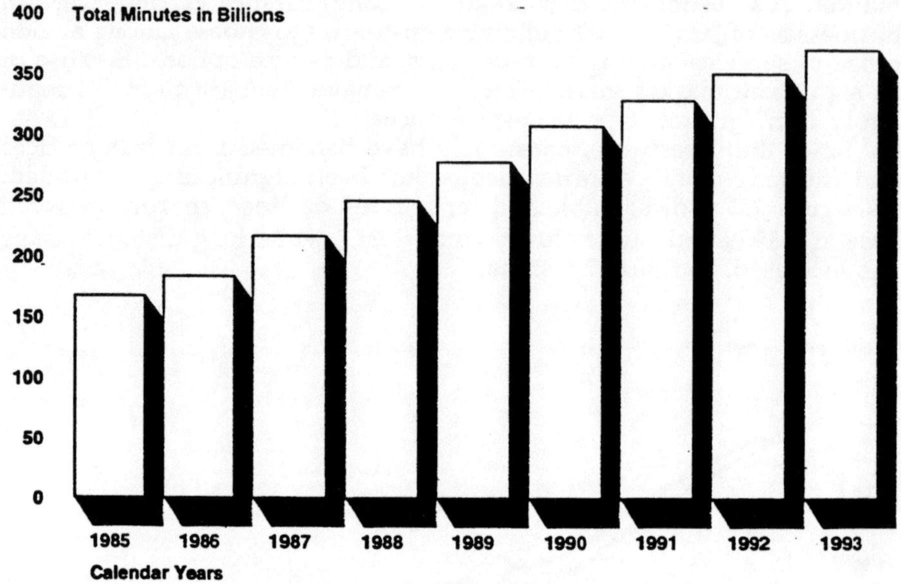

Figure 2.3. Total Long-Distance Usage, 1985-93.

Technological advances and increased competition spurred AT&T, Sprint, and MCI to install all-digital and/or fiber-optic networks. In 1987, AT&T estimated that it would finish installing an all-digital network by 2010. However, after investing $6 billion since 1984, AT&T had completed its installation by 1991. Between 1986 and 1993, the total miles of fiber-optic cable installed by all long-distance companies increased nearly fivefold, from about 20,000 to nearly 100,000, as shown in figure 2.4.

These improvements in the long-distance infrastructure have provided the large capacity that the Information Superhighway could conceivably require. However, local infrastructure will also need to have greater capacity if the Information Superhighway is to reach homes, schools, and businesses. Because the local infrastructure contains many times the route-miles of the long-distance infrastructure contains many times the route-miles of the long-distance infrastructure, these capacity improvements will be more costly. The administration, the Congress and the telecommunications industry agree in principle that competition in the local telecommunications markets would help increase consumer choices, lower prices, and stimulate the required investment, just as it has in the long-distance market.

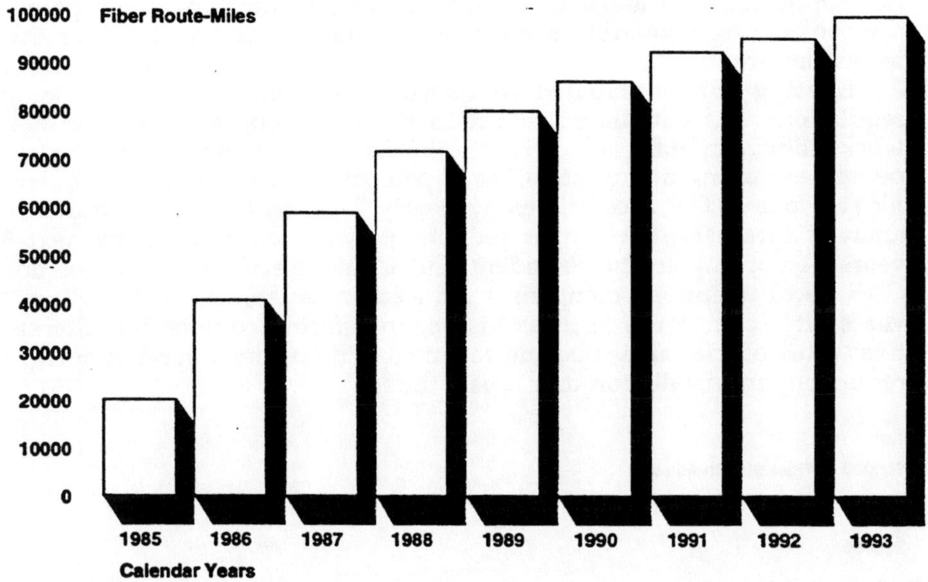

Note: According to FCC, route miles in the long-distance infrastructure are essentially equal to sheath-miles.

Figure 2.4. Miles of Fiber-Optic Cable in the Long Distance Infrastructure, 1985-93.

New Competitors in Local Telephone Service are Stimulating Infrastructure Improvements

Some competition has emerged at the local level. Companies called competitive access providers (CAP) have begun providing businesses with alternatives to the local telephone companies in some markets. These companies use their own local infrastructure and switches to route calls directly to and from the long-distance network, thus bypassing the local telephone companies' access charges. While competition from CAPs is expected to grow, telephone service provided by cable television companies and wireless communications providers - cellular, satellite, and PCS - could also increase competition in the local telephone service market.[7] Finally, some utility companies are installing

[7] Currently, carriers attempting to compete with local telephone companies, or those providing adjunct (e.g., cellular) services, must pay local telephone companies for

fiber-optic cable to assist in demand management.[8] These companies are considering providing some telecommunications services over this infrastructure.

Existing and anticipated competition, as well as relaxed pricing regulations, has stimulated cost reductions and upgrades in local networks. Between 1988 and 1992, the BOCs reduced their operating expenses, excluding depreciation, by 27 percent and cut the number of employees per 10,000 access lines by nearly 7 percent. A recent industry analysis forecasts that similar reductions could occur over the next 5 years. According to the President and Chief Executive Officer of one CAP, local telephone companies reduced in several markets within 2 years after companies such as his began offering competitive alternatives. This official also cited improvements in customer service, such as reductions in installation and repair times.

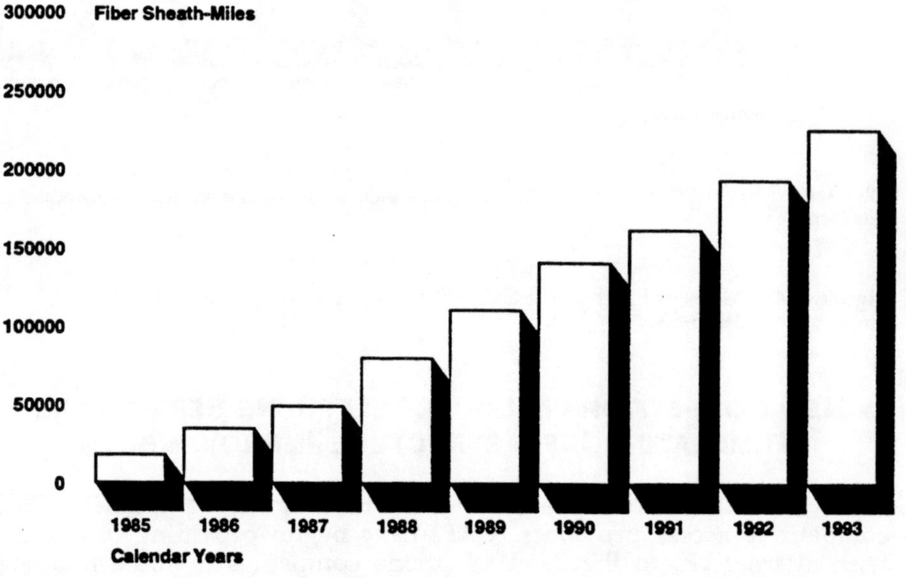

Figure 2.5. Miles of Fiber-Optic Cable Installed by Local Telephone Companies, 1985-93.

---

interconnection when completing calls in the local network. However, local telephone companies do not pay similar access fees when delivering a call to other carriers, such as cellular service providers. This lack of reciprocal pricing could be an obstacle for competitors.

8 Through demand management, utilities encourage consumers to use major appliances during off-peak hours, thereby reducing peak-capacity requirements and deferring the need to build additional power plants.

Local telephone companies have begun installing fiber-optic cable, as figure 2.5 shows. While the total number of fiber sheath-miles in the local telephone infrastructure may appear high compared with the total number of route-miles in the long-distance infrastructure, the local infrastructure is many times larger and more distributed. Consequently, it is more costly to upgrade. As figure 2.6 shows, only 6 percent of the local infrastructure contained fiber-optic cable at the end of 1993. Most of these exist primarily in the central arteries of the local infrastructure and do not extend to residences. To carry the Information Superhighway through a wired network to homes, schools and businesses, high-capacity wires, such as fiber-optic or coaxial cables, will be needed throughout the local infrastructure.[9]

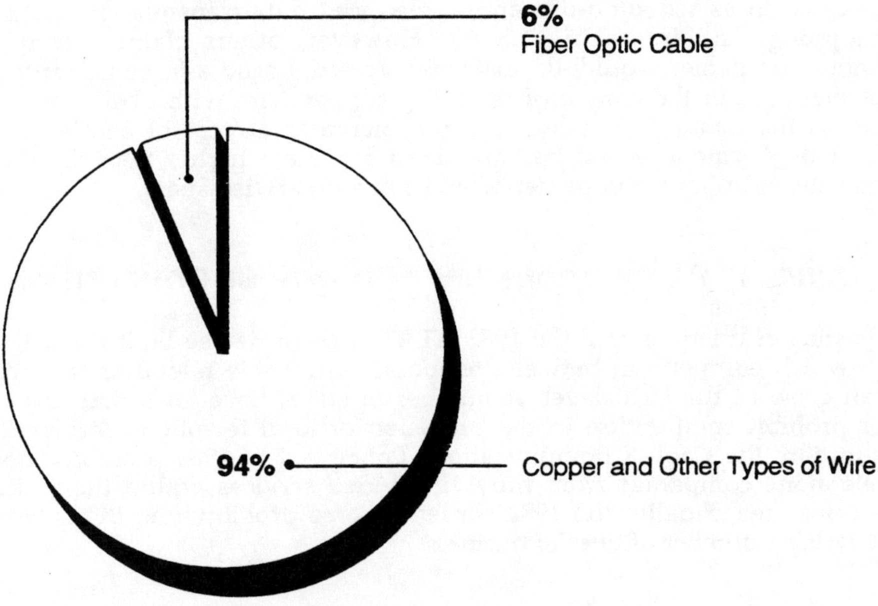

Note: According to FCC, most wire other than fiber-optic cable is copper.

Source: Preliminary Statistics of Communications Common Carriers, FCC, July 5, 1994, Washington, D.C.

Figure 2.6. Fiber-optic cable as a percentage of all wire in the local infrastructure as of December 31, 1993.

[9] Wireless networks, such as PCS, will also have a role in the development of the Information Superhighway.

Additionally, the BOCs and GTE have installed Integrated Services Digital Network (ISDN) technology - which allows the simultaneous transmission of voice and data - in about 25 percent of their local networks, and they have introduced advanced network control functions that permit a multitude of advanced applications in over 63 percent of their networks. These percentages are expected to increase to 45 percent and 90 percent, respectively, by 1996, according to a recent industry analysis. These upgrades will enable these companies to provide advanced services such as caller identification, return call, repeat call, and ultimately, video entertainment.

Cost estimates to fully deploy fiber-optics in the local infrastructure vary widely. Some are as high as $500 billion to upgrade the existing local infrastructure to provide the full range of multimedia services, such as video-on-demand, high-speed data transmissions, home shopping, and interactive games. However, others claim that telephone companies would, on their own accord, spend a large percentage of that sum in the course of replacing copper wire with fiber-optic cable in the coming decades, and the incremental cost of accelerating fiber deployment would be only about 5 percent higher than the total that the telephone companies would have otherwise spent.

Current Restrictions Limit Growth of Competition

Existing restrictions and the 1982 AT&T consent decree limit the extent to which competition between telephone and cable television services can grow at the local level. A number of states have laws that restrict or prohibit competition in the provision of local telephone service. In addition, the Cable Communications Policy Act of 1984 prohibits local telephone companies from providing video services within their local service area. Finally, the 1982 consent decree prohibits the BOCs from entering a number of lines of business.

Many States Prohibit Local Telephone Service Competition

A number of states have laws that prohibit or restrict competition in the provision of local telephone service. According to the National Association of Regulatory Utility Commissioners, 24 states prohibit and another 16 partially restrict local competition. If these restrictions were eliminated, increased local competition could come from a number of sources. The cable television infrastructure could be used to carry telephone service, since it can be upgraded to provide such service and is readily accessible to about 95 percent of U.S. homes. This would allow cable television companies to offer local telephone service in competition with local telephone companies. Additionally, by purchasing cable television companies outside their geographic regions, local telephone companies could begin competing with one another by providing local telephone service through their cable subsidiaries. Similarly, long-distance companies could provide local telephone service through joint ventures with cable companies. Outside the cable infrastructure, CAPs could begin operating in states where local competition had heretofore been prohibited, or companies could build their own local infrastructure, as MCI plans to do.

In general, state laws prohibiting local competition allow regulators to maintain a pricing structure for local telephone service that furthers the goal of universal service - the availability of affordably priced rudimentary telephone service to all Americans.[10] As discussed in chapter 3, many observers believe that states have pursued this goal by requiring the local telephone companies to allocate their costs in such a way that the local telephone company can provide residential and rural telephone service at rates that are below fully distributed costs, while charging rates above fully distributed costs for long-distance access to the local infrastructure and for intrastate long-distance calls. Because greater competition generally leads to prices that are more in accordance with cost considerations, allowing competitors to enter the local telephone market may make the current cost allocation system unworkable. Chapter 3 discusses this issue in more detail.

Cable Regulations Limit Local Telephone Companies' Competitive Options

Some telephone companies want to provide video programming services in competition with local cable companies within their local service area, but existing restrictions generally prevent local telephone companies from doing so. Section 613(b) of the Communications Act of 1934, as amended, generally prohibits local telephone companies from providing video programming over their own systems, either directly or through an affiliate, to subscribers in their telephone service area.[11]

[10] Also, in many states, public utility commissions believe that the local telephone service market is a natural monopoly.

[11] The provisions of video services by a BOC within its service area would also conflict with the AT&T consent decree, since operation of a cable system may involve crossing of its local access and transport area boundaries - the geographic limits of the telephone company's service area. The AT&T consent decree prohibits BOCs from providing service sthat extend beyond these boundaries. While some BOCs have plans to provide video services outside their service areas, these require that the court grant a waiver from the consent decree's provision.

This provision is commonly referred to as the "telco/cable cross-ownership restriction."

The telco/cable cross-ownership restriction had its genesis in a similar restriction imposed by FCC in 1970. At that time, FCC found that local telephone companies had the potential to discriminate against independent cable television providers in favor of their own affiliates in granting access to poles for attaching cable television lines. While the issue of pole access was addressed in major part by the Pole Attachment Act of 1978, FCC noted concern that local telephone companies could hide the costs of providing cable television in their telephone rate structures, a practice called cross-subsidizing. This practice would result in higher telephone rates and increased cash flow from the telephone companies' monopoly telephone service customers, which local telephone companies could then use to underprice cable television competitors, force them out of business, and thus extend their monopolies to cable television.[12]

The 1982 Consent Decree Imposed Line-Of-Business Restrictions on the BOCs

The 1982 AT&T consent decree, approved by the U.S. district court, initially prohibited the BOCS from (1) providing long-distance services, (2) manufacturing or providing telecommunication equipment, (3) manufacturing customer premises equipment, (4) providing information services, and (5) providing nontelecommunications products or services, such as operating a cafeteria on company premises.[13] These restrictions are referred to as line-of-business restrictions.

The court recognized that after divestiture, the BOCS would possess a monopoly over local telephone service in their geographic areas but concluded that this condition alone would not require the BOCS to be barred from all competitive markets. Rather, the court concluded that a line-of-business restriction on the BOCS would be permissible only if there was a substantial possibility that the BOCS would use their monopoly power to impede competition in a particular market. Two relevant factors were considered: (1) whether the BWS would actually have the incentive and opportunity to act anticompetitively and (2) whether the participation of the BOCS would contribute to the creation of a competitive market. In addition, the court also considered

[12] Federal and state regulations attempt to ensure that costs associated with any nonregulated services (such as information services) are not allocated to regulated local telephone service. However, as the regulatory process is complex and confronts many uncertainties, not all inappropriate cost shfting can be uncovered by regulators.

[13] The restriction on nontelecommunication products or services was lifted in 1987, and the prohibition on providing information was lifted in 1991.

important public policies, such as the effects of the restrictions on the rates for local telephone services. Applying this analysis, the court found the five previously noted restrictions to be warranted.

The court recognized, however, that over time it was probable that the BOCS would lose the ability to leverage their monopoly power in competitive markets. Accordingly, the court required that the decree explicitly provide a mechanism for removing line-of-business restrictions. The competitive entry test imposed by the modified consent decree provides for the removal of a line-of-business restriction upon a showing "that there is no substantial possibility that [a BOC] could use its monopoly power to impede competition in the market it seeks to enter."

SOME COMPETITIVE BARRIERS HAVE BEEN ELIMINATED, WHILE OTHERS HAVE BEEN QUESTIONED

States, FCC, and the courts have taken a number of actions that have affected telecommunications.

- Some states have changed their laws to allow more local telephone competition in recent years, and others are considering such changes.
- FCC reevaluated its cable cross-ownership policy, noting that the cable television industry has achieved substantial growth and that the potential benefits of increased competition outweighed the risk of anticompetitive behavior. In 1992, FCC recommended that the Congress remove the statutory provision against local telephone companies providing video services, subject to appropriate safeguards.
- Two district courts have ruled that the cable cross-ownership restriction is an unconstitutional burden on the telephone companies' right to free speech under the First Amendment.[14]
- The U.S. district court removed the BOCS' restriction on providing nontelecommunications products and services in 1987 and information services in 1991.[15]

---

14 See, *U.S. West Inc. v. United States,* No. C93-1523R (W.D. Wash. June 15, 1994); *Chesapeake & Potomac Tel. Co. v. United States,* 830 F. Supp. 909 (E.D. Va. 1993).

15 In *U.S. v. Western Elec. Co.,* 900 F.2d 283, 305 (D.C. Cir. 1990), the court of appeals concluded that the consent decree's test for removing line-of-business restrictios applied only to contested modifications. For uncontested modifications - when all the parties to an agreement agree to the lifting of a restriction - the court found that a public interest test is

House and Senate Have Proposed Legislation

Recognizing that technological advances have eroded and will continue to erode the distinctions between the competitive and noncompetitive segments of the telecommunications industry, the Congress is considering legislation aimed at encouraging competition while protecting consumers from monopolistic pricing practices as the transition to competition occurs. The House passed H.R. 3626 - The Antitrust and Communications Reform Act of 1994 and H.R. 3636, the National Communications Competition and Information Infrastructure Act of 1994 - on June 28, 1994 and combined these into one bill, numbered and titled as the former. Senate bill S. 1822—The Communications Act of 1994 has been reported out of the Committee on Commerce, Science, and Transportation but as of September 23, 1994, had not reached the Senate floor for consideration.

The bills, among other things, provide the conditions that must be met before a BOC can provide long-distance services; allow telephone companies to offer video programming services in their market areas under specific conditions and safeguards; provide requirements for the FCC to establish procedures to ensure preservation of the principle of universal service; preempt state and local laws that prohibit telecommunications competition; and provide requirements for interconnection and nondiscriminatory access to telecommunications facilities and equipment. Appendix III provides highlights of selected provisions of these bills.

Market Power of Local Telephone Companies Presents Challenges in Fostering Competition

The proposed telecommunications legislation has generated intense debate over whether and to what extent consumers will need protection from the local telephone companies' potentially anticompetitive use of market power. A central issue in the debate is whether the recent emergence of CAPS provides sufficient competition to safely remove the existing controls on the BOCS and if not, what conditions would indicate that sufficient competition exists and what safeguards would be needed to protect consumers from the BOCS' market power. The BOCS raised the issue of regulatory parity, claiming that if state regulations are modified to allow long-distance, cable television, or other businesses to provide local telephone service, the BOCS should be allowed similar flexibility. The BOCS claim that the local telephone

appropriate. Because the removal of the information services restriction was uncontested, the court specified that the public interest standard be applied to remove this restriction.

market is already competitive, citing the increasing presence of CAPS and potential competition from cable television companies and long-distance companies offering local telephone service.

On the other hand, a recent industry analysis reported that CAPs the major current source of local competition—have attracted only about $260 million out of $27 billion in long-distance access business. Consequently, long-distance companies argue that the BOCS dominate the local market nearly as much as they did in 1984 when the consent decree was implemented, and therefore more competition at the local level is needed before the BOCS can be allowed to provide long-distance services.

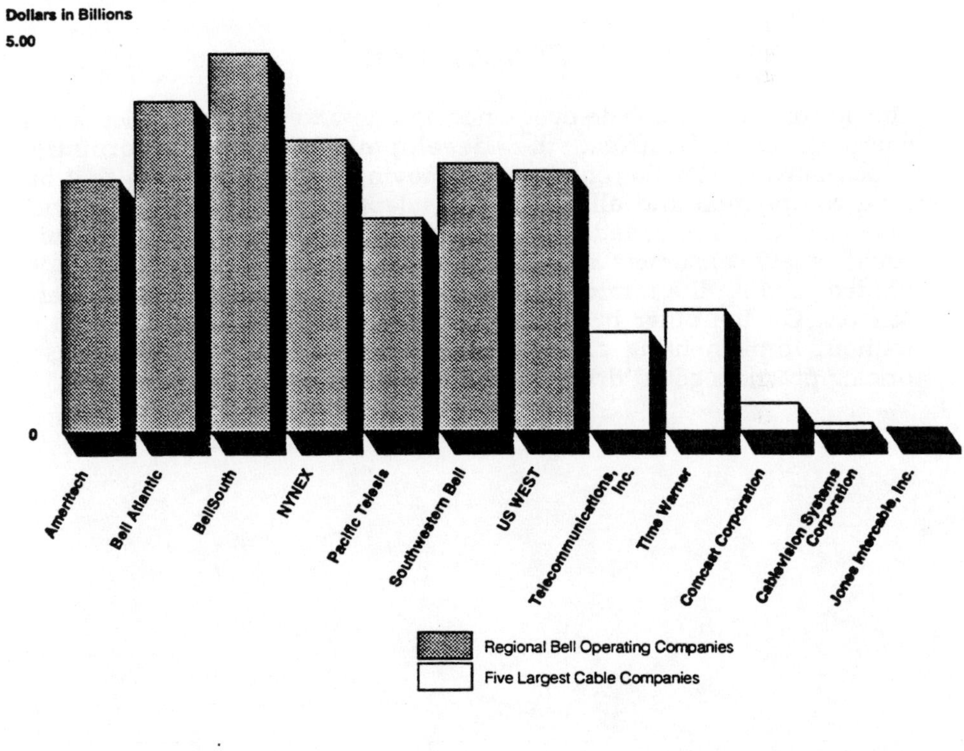

Figure 2.7. 1993 cash flow of regional bell operating companies and the five largest cable companies

In addition, other groups, including the cable television industry, have cited the strong financial position of the seven regional Bell operating companies. The regional companies' ready access to cash, relative to that of cable companies, could provide them with a competitive advantage in making the required investment to provide diversified services. As figure 2.7 shows, the regional companies' 1993 cash flow, defined as the cash received from customers minus the cash paid for operating expenses, ranged from $2.7 billion to $4.8 billion. Most of this cash flow was invested in capital. In contrast, the financial position of the five largest cable companies - likely future competitors of the BOC - was not nearly as strong. While Telecommunications, Inc., and Time Warner had 1993 cash flows of $1.25 billion and $1.53 billion,[16] respectively, the combined cash flow of the remaining three cable companies totaled only $470 million.[17]

CONCLUSIONS

The outcome of the debate over when and how to remove restrictions on competition will affect the development of the Information Superhighway. On the one hand, removing state regulations that bar local competition and allowing local telephone companies to provide video services in competition with the local cable television companies could benefit consumers and accelerate the local infrastructure upgrades needed to bring the Information Superhighway to homes, business, and schools. On the other hand, removing regulations either too soon or without implementing adequate safeguards to prevent monopolistic pricing practices could drive out rather than encourage competition.

---

[16] About 85 percent of Time Warner's $1.53 billion operating revenues are from noncable sources.

[17] *Telecommunication: Financial Information on 16 Telephone and Cable Companies* (GAO/RCED/AIMD-94-221FS, July 8, 1994).

Chapter 3

COMPETITION AND TECHNOLOGY AFFECT UNIVERSAL SERVICE

The prospect of competition in the local telephone service market, as well as advances in telecommunications technology, require that several decisions be made about universal service the long-standing public policy goal that affordable rudimentary telephone service be accessible to all individuals. These decisions involve (1) procedural issues concerning how to fund universal service in a more competitive environment and (2) value judgments on whether and how the package of services included under the universal service and universal access umbrella should be broadened.

FUNDING MECHANISM FOR UNIVERSAL SERVICE WILL NEED REVISION IN A COMPETITIVE ENVIRONMENT

Currently, universal service is provided through a complex system of implicit and explicit subsidies provided through the federal and state regulatory process and through federally managed programs. However, because the majority of universal service funding comes from services that, through the state regulatory process, are priced above fully distributed costs, the funding process could break down as competitors price these services lower than the incumbent telephone company.

Various Policies and Programs Help Fund Universal Service

Federal and state regulators have developed a system of cost allocation and recovery that keeps residential and rural rates at affordable levels in order to meet the objective of universal service—providing everyone with access to affordable rudimentary telephone service. Since the rate-making process has traditionally been based on the cost of providing services, many observers believe that rates for local residential and rural service would be higher than existing levels if based on fully distributed costs. Federal and state regulators have maintained low rates for these services through a system that allocates some local telephone infrastructure costs to other services.

Historically, FCC and state regulators worked with AT&T and other local telephone companies to establish affordable local residential rates by allocating some of the cost of the local infrastructure to inter- and intrastate long-distance service. Because fewer costs were allocated to local telephone service, rates were held at lower levels than would have otherwise been the case. After divestiture, the pricing mechanism used to fund low local residential and rural rates became more complex as regulators were now dealing with many more companies providing service in numerous market segments of the telephone industry. However, the key elements of providing affordable local residential and rural telephone service continued to involve cost allocation and recovery as in the pre-divestiture era.

Today, as before the divestiture, regulators require the local telephone companies to allocate some of the costs of the local telephone infrastructure to other services. The following summarizes two major ways that cost allocation occurs.

- FCC's policies require long distance companies to pay to the local telephone companies a per-minute Carrier Common Line Charge (access fee). These revenues are used to recover part of the costs of the local telephone infrastructure that are assigned to interstate long-distance service. Because many local infrastructure costs do not vary with actual usage, charging per-minute fees amounts to pricing access above fully distributed cost. A 1994 industry analysis estimated that long-distance access charges were between 35 percent and 60 percent above cost-based pricing levels, while residential and rural local-service rates were 35 percent to 40 percent below what they would be under cost-based prices.[18]
- Regulators in many states allocate a significant portion of the cost of the local telephone infrastructure to intrastate long-distance services. This practice results in above-cost rates for access fees and per-minute usage on these types of calls, thereby helping to provide affordable rural and residential telephone service.

[18] A result of charging prices that are higher than fully distributed cost is that consumers will choose to use less of the services than is economically efficient.

While the above noted programs provide a large share of the cost of providing affordable residential and rural telephone service, several other federal and state policies and programs help to promote universal service. A brief description of some of these programs follows.

- The Universal Service Fund assists "high-cost" local telephone companies, which the FCC defines as those that have an average cost per access line exceeding 115 percent of the national average. The fund helps these high-cost companies (that tend to be located in rural areas) to provide local telephone service at rates that are similar to national averages. The Universal Service Fund is supported by fees levied on long-distance carriers according to the number of customers choosing their company for long-distance service.
- FCC administers two programs aimed at providing direct subsidies to low-income individuals. The Link-up Program helps offset low-income subscribes' initial installation costs and encourages telephone companies to offer installment payments. The Lifeline Program helps defray the cost of monthly service for low-income residents by waiving up to $3.50 of the federal monthly subscriber line charge. Eligibility criteria for these programs vary from state to state.
- The Rural Electrification Administration, Department of Agriculture, provides low-cost loans and loan guarantees to rural telephone companies and cooperatives.

Revised Funding Mechanism is Needed

If competition in the local telephone service market is allowed, new procedures will be required to ensure the continuation of universal service. While inter- and intrastate long-distance access charges and intrastate long-distance rates have traditionally provided the major source of funds used to keep residential and rural rates low, competitors are likely to compete primarily for heavy users of inter- and intrastate long-distance services in states where regulations permit local competition. Currently, these competitors have no obligation to provide or contribute toward the provision of local residential and rural telephone service. Local telephone companies believe that losing this source of funds to provide universal service could place a financial strain on high-cost companies and on some subscribers. Hence, as competition becomes more widespread, a revised funding mechanism for universal service is required.

Current System of Allocating Universal Service Subsidies Questioned

An additional issue that policy makers will need to consider is how to distribute subsidies. Currently, cost allocation mechanisms and other programs designed to further universal service are based primarily on the pricing of different types of services and on the cost structure of providers (i.e., residential service and high-cost telephone companies), rather than on an individual subscriber's ability to pay. Consequently, subsidies may not go where they are most needed.

While over 94 percent of U.S. residences had telephone service in 1993, the distribution varies according to household income. For example, while more than 99 percent of households with incomes over $40,000 had telephone service, less than 90 percent with incomes under $10,000 had service, and only 73 percent of households with incomes below $5,000 had service. Some industry observers have pointed out that a means test should be used as the principal criterion to allocate universal service subsidies.

Questions Exist About Whether and Which Additional Services Should Be Provided or Universally Accessible

The Information Superhighway could make available a host of advanced services to businesses, schools, medical centers, and the population at large. Redefining universal service in this new environment raises questions on two levels. First, what advanced services should be provided to everyone? Second, what, if any, additional services should be accessible to everyone as options?

Decisions are Required on What Services Should be Universally Provided

Currently, universal service consists of rudimentary telephone service, the definition of which has evolved over time. Initially, rudimentary service was considered a multi-party line. Gradually, the number of parties decreased until today, single-party lines are standard. In some locations, touch-tone service has been included in rudimentary telephone service.

As the Information Superhighway develops, a vastly expanded array of telecommunications services could become available. For example, consumers may have on-line access to health care information, allowing them to become more actively involved in their own health care, thereby reducing unnecessarily visits to the doctor. Consumers could also have better access to government information and services. While these services could benefit society, building the infrastructure to provide these expanded services to every home in America will be costly—up to $500 billion by some estimates and some question exists as to which services the average citizen needs or wants. Although a recent survey indicated significant consumer demand for interactive services, the survey also showed that over 40 percent of the respondents in the households surveyed were either undecided or unwilling to pay for additional services.

In addition to facing infrastructure costs, consumers may need new appliances to access Information Superhighway services. For access to rudimentary telephone service, only a telephone was required. Those accessing the Information Superhighway's services may need a personal computer, interactive television, or other wired or wireless devices, in addition to a conventional telephone. These appliances are not commonly found in homes of the economically disadvantaged. Providing the required appliances to those who cannot otherwise afford them will increase the cost of providing universal service.

Decisions Needed on Whether Services Should be Universally Available as Options

An additional issue is determining which Information Superhighway services should be universally accessible as options, beyond those services made available to everyone under universal service. To make these services available, infrastructure improvements may be required beyond those required to provide universal service. However, these costs could be mitigated, depending on how decision makers define "availability." Additional services could be deemed available if consumers can obtain them at central locations, such as at a public library, which would be less costly than making them available to every home. Whatever the results of these decisions, consumers would ultimately pay the cost of providing the required infrastructure. However, the installation and appliance costs, if needed to receive optional services, would probably not be subsidized.

CONCLUSIONS

The prospect of greater competition in the local telephone services market raises the question of how to maintain the pricing structures that help to promote universal service. Some form of funding for universal service, supported by providers of telecommunications services, is probably appropriate. A more difficult issue, however, is determining which telecommunications services should be provided as part of the universal service package, which should be available as options, and how to pay for them. Providing Information Superhighway services to all schools, hospitals, and libraries would provide social benefits that could justify some of the cost. However, building the infrastructure needed to make every Information Superhighway service available to every home and business would be costly, and not everyone may need or desire every service.

Chapter 4

INFORMATION SUPERHIGHWAY POSES TECHNICAL CHALLENGES

The success of the Information Superhighway will also depend on how well industry and government address several technical challenges. An effective Information Superhighway requires technology that can ensure (1) security, privacy, and reliability and (2) the smooth flow of information and provide number portability—the freedom to change carriers without changing telephone numbers.[19] A systems perspective is needed to ensure that these challenges are addressed in a coordinated fashion.

TECHNOLOGICAL ADVANCES POSE CHALLENGES TO SECURITY, PRIVACY AND RELIABILITY

Concentrated data bases, widely distributed networks, and the increasing sophistication of criminals pose threats to computer security and information privacy. Advances in communications and data encryption technologies hamper federal law enforcement efforts, while federal efforts to address this issue have caused controversy. Concentrated data bases also heighten the need for ensuring reliability, since the failure of a single component of a system can render millions of records inaccessible.

---

19 While we recognize that intellectual propert rights also pose significant issues for telecommunications decision makers, we did not address this area. The Information Infrastructure Task Force, chaired by the Secretary of Commerce, is preparing a report focusing on copyright law and its application and effectiveness in the context of the Information Superhighway.

Security Threat Has Increased

While information security has long been an important issue, a number of factors increase the risks in today's electronic age. First, electronic record keeping concentrates large volumes of data in a single location, thereby rendering the consequences of unauthorized access more severe. Second, networked computers widely disperse electronic traffic, increasing the potential for unauthorized intercept. Third, criminals are gaining technical skills that enable them to foil sophisticated security systems.

Attacks against the Internet illustrate potential vulnerabilities. In 1988, a worm—a malignant computer program that reproduces itself automatically—invaded the Internet and denied service to thousands of people working at the nation's major research centers. Again, in 1994, intruders managed to obtain the names and passwords of 100,000 people who use the Internet at certain locations and to conceal the theft.

The Department of Defense's Advanced Research Projects Agency has established a Computer Emergency Response Team to help the Internet community respond to attacks. This and other incident response teams now serve as focal points for identifying security vulnerabilities. While response teams can identify problems and recommend corrective action, the manufacturers and network users themselves are responsible for taking action. To ensure security on the Information Superhighway, additional procedures will be required to accurately identify the users, verify their authority to access information, and prevent malicious interference with software programs or modification of data files.

Privacy Needs to be Ensured

Systems for protecting privacy should enable individuals to determine when, how, and to what extent personal information is collected and used. However, if not properly implemented and managed, the technologies that provide the means to manage massive volumes of personal information also increase the risk that this information may be abused. This risk is heightened by

- the widespread use of common identifiers, such as Social Security numbers, to select, track, and link electronic records;
- the dramatic increase in the number of widely interconnected systems, which increases opportunities for unauthorized access;
- the growth of large data bases and the increasing sophistication of applications that allow the rapid matching of millions of records and the development of detailed computer profiles on individuals; and

- the increasing sophistication of computer criminals and their growing ability to secretly penetrate computer systems and retrieve massive amounts of confidential information.

Today's patchwork of information privacy laws, practices, and technical safeguards may fall short of ensuring the privacy of personal information maintained in thousands of widely interconnected government and private computer systems. In 1990, we reported that in over 900 of the largest federal computer systems containing privacy data, 11 percent did not require user authentication, 40 percent had no intrusion detection controls, and 6 percent had no access controls.[20] A lack of such controls can lead to egregious abuses. For example, in 1993 we reported that scores of Internal Revenue Service employees had accessed the agency's data bases to issue fraudulent refunds or had browsed the taxpayer accounts of friends, relatives, neighbors, and celebrities.[21]

Recognizing that personal data need better protection, the administration's Information Infrastructure Task Force is studying the issue. A working group has identified a number of tasks, including (1) scoping the nature of the privacy problem; (2) developing a statement of fair information practices and determining the responsible organizations and individuals; and (3) identifying gaps in existing laws, recommending changes, and drafting legislation, if necessary.

Technology Could Impair Law Enforcement and Intelligence Capabilities

Sophisticated encryption prevents third parties, including law enforcement and intelligence agencies, from monitoring encrypted messages, while digital communication makes wiretapping increasingly difficult. The federal government is attempting to address these issues, but its efforts to date have generated considerable controversy. The government's strategy includes (1) a major new federal encryption initiative known as the "Clipper Chip," recently renamed the "Key Encryption Standard," to facilitate court-ordered wiretapping and (2) proposed legislation that would ensure that telecommunication equipment and services can meet law enforcement's wiretapping requirements.

---

20 *Computers and Privacy: How the Government Obtains, Verifies, Uses, and Protects Personal Data* (GAO/IMTEC-90-70BR, Aug. 3, 1990).

21 *IRS Information Systems: Weaknesses Increase Risk of Fraud and Impair Reliability of Management Information* (GAO/AIMD-93-34, Sept. 22, 1993).

Efforts to Decipher Encrypted Messages are Controversial

To enable federal authorities to decrypt intercepted messages, the federal government is seeking the computer hardware industry's voluntary cooperation to install the Clipper Chip in all its telephone communications hardware. The chip contains a unique key that is used to encrypt and decrypt messages. This unique key is then split into two components and delivered to government agencies, acting as escrow agents, for safekeeping. To decipher information encoded using the Clipper Chip in the course of court-authorized wiretapping, federal authorities can obtain the unique key from the escrow agents.

The Clipper Chip initiative has generated considerable controversy within the information industry. According to the Computer System Security and Privacy Advisory Board, created by the Congress in 1987 to advise the Secretary of Commerce and the Director of the National Institute of Standards and Technology on security and privacy issues, the federal government has not (1) clearly articulated the problem that the Clipper Chip attempts to resolve, (2) considered other potential alternatives, or (3) fully examined the chip's legal and economic implications.

In response to the controversy, the administration is reviewing its policy on the Clipper Chip. The administration stated that the Clipper Chip would not be used for computer or video networks and expressed a willingness to work with computer industry representatives and privacy advocates to design a system more acceptable to all.

New Legislation Would Require Wiretap Capability in Telecommunications Devices

Recognizing that new telecommunications devices can be developed that are invulnerable to court-ordered wiretaps, a bill has been introduced that would, among other things, generally require communications carriers to deploy equipment and services that can accommodate law enforcement needs. The bill would require that a communications carrier's equipment and services allow law enforcement personnel to intercept a subscriber's communications and obtain reasonably available call-identifying information about the origin and destination of communications. Because subjects of wiretaps on mobile communications devices may cross carrier boundaries, the bill would require that a carrier inform government personnel of the identity of the carrier to whom the signal was transferred. The bill would authorize $500 million over 4 years for the Department of Justice to reimburse telecommunications carriers for expenses that they incur in complying with these requirements.

Assurance of Reliability is Needed

As more and more telecommunications traffic is concentrated in fewer, high-capacity channels, a failure by any one element of the Information Superhighway could become increasingly damaging. For example, in June 1991 two separate telephone outages at opposite ends of the country eliminated local telephone service to 8 million people and affected emergency services. A few months later, AT&T suffered a massive outage in New York City that cut most long-distance telephone communications to and from the city as well as air traffic to the area's major airports. FCC noted that this outage resulted in significant loss of the Federal Aviation Administration's radar sites, radio channels, and computer links. This resulted in 1,174 canceled or delayed flights and about 85,000 inconvenienced passengers. More than 7 hours passed before full service was restored.[22]

The federal government and industry have undertaken a variety of efforts to improve the reliability of telecommunications systems. For example, FCC formed the Network Reliability Council following serious network outages in 1991. Additionally, the administration's Information Infrastructure Task Force has formed a network reliability working group, and industry has developed a number of mutual aid and restoration agreements to permit the temporary sharing of resources and rerouting of information traffic and services through other systems.

Added attention to system reliability will be required, however, as the Information Superhighway grows to its full potential. Although mutual aid agreements exist, the current approach relies primarily on individual carriers to manage their own networks. As the telecommunications industry grows more competitive, these arrangements may prove inadequate. Additionally, the diversity of products and operators on the Information Superhighway may increase the difficulty of diagnosing and correcting problems.

Interoperability is Required

Interoperability—defined as the ability of two systems to transfer information easily—will be critical to establishing the "seamless web" of networks and equipment envisioned for the Information Superhighway. Number portability, which would allow consumers to switch telecommunications carriers without changing their telephone numbers, is a second aspect of interoperability that will be important to the success of the superhighway.

---

22 *Telecommunications: Interruptions of Telephone Service* (GAO/RCED-93-79FS, Mar. 5, 1993).

Equipment and Systems Interoperability is Required

A seamless web of equipment and networks would allow equipment and systems, manufactured by different companies and using different technologies, to transfer information without delay. Complete interoperability would, for example, allow a social worker in Appalachia to prepare a message on a lap-top computer and transmit it via wireless technology to a receiver. From there, the message might be carried over wires to a satellite earth station, beamed up to a satellite, and beamed back to earth in San Francisco. The message might then be sent over wires to a broadcast television station and then, ultimately, to the addressee's interactive television. The addressee might respond to the message via the reverse route.

Each component of the Information Superhighway—the lap-top computers, wire infrastructures and switches, satellites, television stations, and interactive televisions—will likely be built by a variety of private concerns. The success of the Information Superhighway will hinge on the ability of these technologies to transfer information easily and accurately, allowing voice, video, and data to flow unimpeded throughout the network.

Some Information Superhighway Facilities Lack Interoperability

Interoperability problems have surfaced in today's information technology. For example, as the BOCS implemented their Integrated Services Digital Networks (ISDN), interoperability problems developed because each BOC had purchased equipment built to differing standards from different suppliers.[23] Videoconferencing also faces interoperability problems because over a dozen incompatible videoconferencing systems are currently on the market. While these systems can interoperate to a degree, certain incompatibilities degrade the picture's quality and preclude the use of advanced features. In the future, interoperability problems are likely to continue, since many of the emerging, sophisticated technologies that are expected to play a role in the Information Superhighway, such as asynchronous transfer mode (ATM),[24] have not realized an acceptable level of interoperability.

---

23 ISDN allows the simultaneous use of telephone lines for transmitting data and voice. (See app. I for a detailed explanation of ISDN.)

24 See appendix I for a detailed description of ATM and other advanced telecommunications technologies.

Some Efforts are Under Way to Promote Interoperability

The private sector and the National Institute of Standards and Technology are addressing ISDN interoperability problems. Additionally, a consortium of government agencies, industry, and academia has formed the Nations Information Infrastructure Test Bed to develop standards and test applications in a wide variety of fields, including health care, mineral and gas exploration, education, and entertainment. Finally, the Alliance for Telecommunications Industry Solutions (formerly called the Exchange Carriers' Standards Association) has formed an ad hoc committee to develop product interoperability tests. The test methodology is available to the industry for use whenever new hardware or software emerges on the market.

Interoperability of Developing Technology is Not Yet Assured

If data, voice, and video are to move unimpeded over the Information Superhighway, further work will be required to ensure interoperability. For example, the Alliance's ad hoc committee addressed only one facet of the Information Superhighway. The committee considered intra-network, product-to-product, and stand-alone equipment modeling and testing to be outside its charter. Other aspects of existing networks, such as interoperability testing requirements for newer technologies, were also not addressed. The Information Superhighway will likely consist of many systems and subsystems, developed by a variety of private sector entities, each with its own—often proprietary—set of standards.

Superhighway Presents Telephone Numbering Challenges

Development of a telephone numbering system that is interchangeable among telecommunications carriers will be important to the development of the Information Superhighway. Consumers' ability to change carriers without changing telephone numbers will play a critical role in developing competition, which, as discussed in chapter 2, will be a key element in spurring development of the Information Superhighway. Number portability, as the concept is called, requires that subscribers, rather than physical locations, be assigned a permanent personal telephone number that would not change if the subscriber changed carriers. While such a system was developed for commercial "800" numbers, no such numbering system has yet been devised for individuals.

Bellcore[25] plans to implement an expanded numbering system in 1995 that would vastly increase the quantity of available telephone numbers. The additional numbers would facilitate the assignment of numbers to individuals and could allow them to switch carriers without changing numbers. However, no entity is currently developing the data base architecture required to implement the system. Bellcore, the entity that has administered the telephone numbering system, plans to relinquish its voluntary performance of this task as soon as FCC finds a replacement.

CONCLUSIONS

If the Information Superhighway is to be successful, privacy, security, reliability, interoperability, and numbering systems must be addressed from a systems perspective. Individuals, governments, and businesses will not use the superhighway without assurances of security, privacy, and a reasonable expectation of reliability. The superhighway cannot function as a seamless web without interoperability. To permit individuals to switch carriers without changing telephone numbers, data bases are required that have yet to be developed. The Information Superhighway will be developed by a number of diverse entities, none of which are likely to be in a position to address these challenges from a systems standpoint. Some mechanism will be needed to ensure that all the challenges are met to allow the Information Superhighway to function as planned. We will examine these and other issues in greater detail in a forthcoming report.

25 Bell Communications Research, also known as Bellcore, is a research organization funded by the BOCs.

Appendix I

TELECOMMUNICATIONS

Advances in telecommunications technology are driving many of the changes occurring in the telecommunications industry today. Because many readers may not be familiar with this technology, this appendix provides a general overview of the technological developments in the field. In addition, this report contains a glossary of telecommunications terms.

Telecommunications is the electronic transmission of information of any type, such as data, television pictures, sound, and facsimile. Telecommunications frequently involves the use of a network, which is a group of interconnected communications facilities and devices used to transmit information. Examples of telecommunications networks include the telephone networks, the television broadcast networks, the Internet "network of networks," and private corporate computer networks.

NETWORK CAPACITY

Current telecommunications networks are designed to transmit one or more of three types of information - audio, video, and/or other types of digital information, such as text - each of which places different demands on the underlying network. These demands differ in terms of the "space" required on a network and how the space is used. The space requirement is called the bandwidth and the ability of a network to accommodate bandwidth is called its transmission capacity. Conversational telephone audio traffic requires a transmission capacity of about 64,000 digital bits per second (referred to as 64 kilobits per second). Additionally, telephone audio traffic requires uninterrupted interactive processing, meaning that the signals must travel quickly between the sender and receiver without unacceptable delays.

In contrast, video transmission requires significantly more capacity than does audio or data transmission. For example, digital television needs a transmission channel with an uncompressed capacity[26] of at least 30 million bits per second (referred to as 30 megabits per second), which is over 450 times the capacity required for telephone conversation. However, video transmissions are generally not interactive and also require uninterrupted operation. Text traffic, such as electronic mail, generally does not require real-time processing and can therefore run at a variety of speeds, depending on the capacity of the network

Analog Versus Digital Signal Format

Electronically transmitted information is sent in either a digital or an analog format As figure I.1 shows, electronic analog signals are continuous electromagnetic waves, while digital signals are usually represented by ones and zeroes.

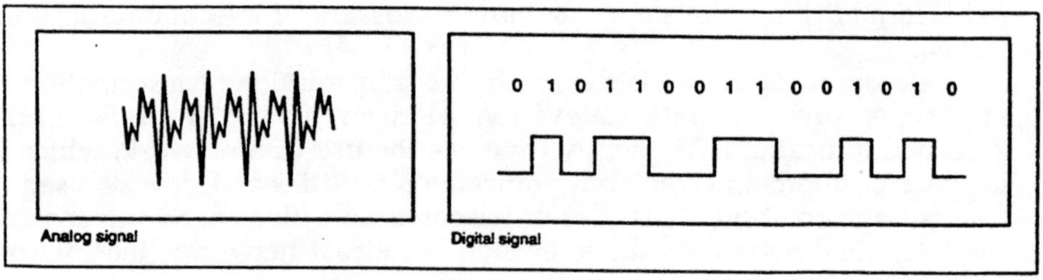

Figure I.1: Analog and digital signals

Historically, most signals have been sent in an analog format. However, the digital format is gaining favor because it offers cost, transmission, and quality control advantages. For example, traditional television broadcasts have been transmitted in an analog format, but the emerging direct broadcast satellite telecasts will be sent to the home in a digital format.[27]

---

26 Compression allows the transmission of data using less capacity.

27 Direct-broadcast satellite transmissions will be sent to residences as digital signals and then changes into analog signals for viewing on standard televisions.

TELECOMMUNICATIONS PROTOCOLS

All electronic signals digital or analog—must be transmitted in an organized manner to ensure that the communications devices in a network send and receive the signals accurately and efficiently. Therefore, transmission devices employ "communication protocols" that establish rules for organizing the transmitted signals. Different protocols have emerged as standards for each particular type of network. These standards can emerge by virtue of their widespread acceptance or they may be developed by an influential group and then adopted by the industry for its products. For example, the Transmission Control Protocol/Internet Protocol has become the Internet standard through its widespread acceptance, while the National Television System Committee developed the U.S. television standard, which FCC and the industry adopted. These differing communications standards can create interoperability problems when attempting to connect different types of networks. For example, although television sets and computer screens both provide video displays, these displays are not interoperable because televisions use an analog display standard, while most computers use a digital display standard.

TELECOMMUNICATIONS TRANSMISSION MEDIA

All signals, whether digital or analog, travel via some type of medium to reach their destinations. The predominant electronic transmission media are copper "twisted pair" wire, coaxial wire, fiber-optic cable, and over-the-air signals. Figure I.2 shows the advantages and disadvantages of each type of medium.

NETWORK SWITCHING

The four previously mentioned media are components of networks. Many networks also use switching and routing devices to send signals to their intended destinations. Circuit switching and packet switching are common switching designs. In a circuit-switching network (see fig. I.3), as in a traditional telephone network, a connection is made at a switching center that physically connects the calling and receiving parties and maintains this connection for as long as needed. No other audio, text, or video information can be sent over this circuit as long as the connection remains intact.

Medium	Advantages	Disadvantages
Copper Twisted Pair Wire 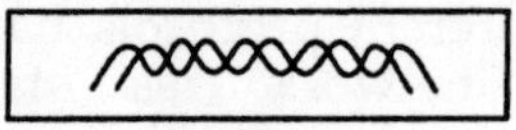	• Is used extensively in residential telephone systems • Is inexpensive • Is widespread	• Has low information capacity • Is susceptible to electronic interference
Coaxial Cable 	• Is used extensively for cable TV • Accessible to 95 percent of U.S. households • Has sufficient capacity to handle most advanced telecommunications applications likely to be used in residences	• Is used primarily in one-way TV networks • Will require additional switching equipment in most cable TV networks to permit two-way communication
Fiber Optic Cable 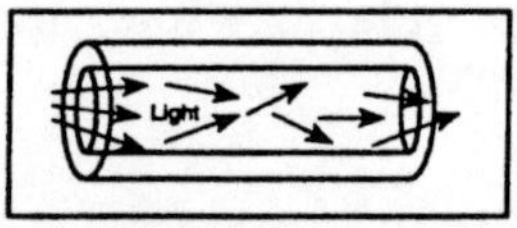	• Has very high information capacity • Is relatively secure • Is not susceptible to electronic interference	• Is expensive to install supporting equipment • Not installed in most residential areas
Over-the-Air 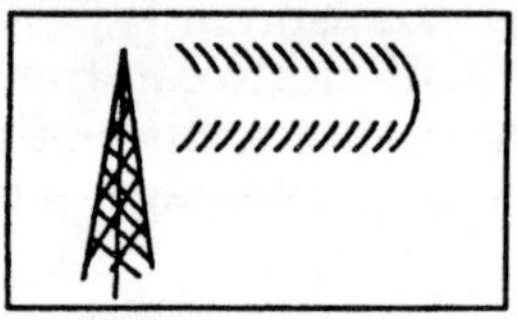	• Enhances mobility • Does not require wire conduits	• Is relatively unsecure • Requires allocation of the frequency spectrum, a finite resource • Is susceptible to electronic interference

Figure I.2: Transmission media and their advantages and disadvantages

In a packet-switching network, such as the Internet, digital data are organized into "packets" and sent through a computer network along the best route available between the source and the destination. A transmitted file, for example, may be broken up into many packets, and these packets may take different paths across the network and then be reassembled at their destination. For most applications, a packet-switching network is more efficient than a circuit-switching network because many datapackets sources may use the same communications line simultaneously (see fig. I.4). However, a circuit-switching network tends to have more consistent performance than a packet-switching network because there is no competition from other communications devices using the line.

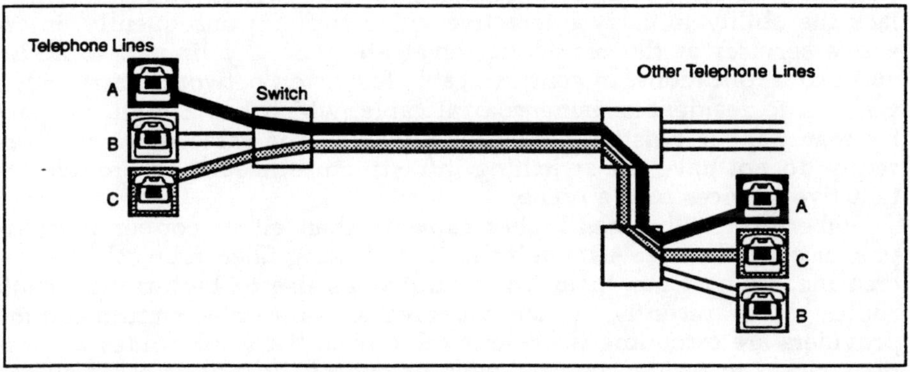

Figure I.3. Representation of a Circuit-Switching Network

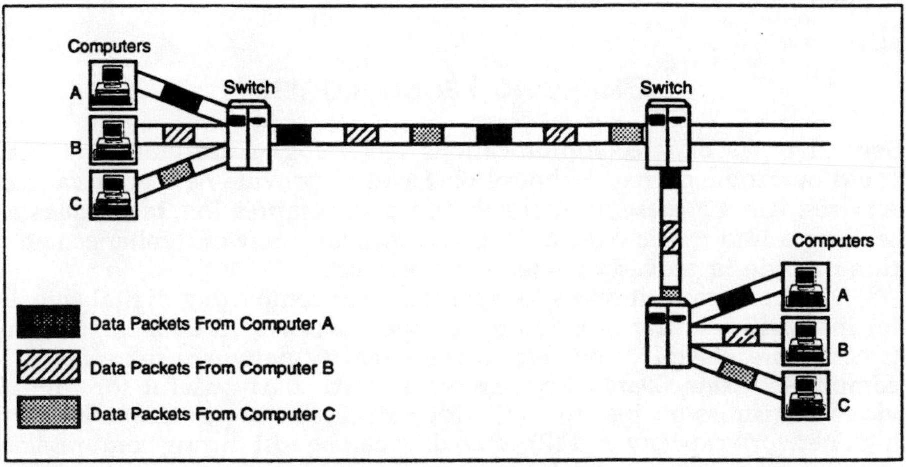

Figure I.4: Representation of a Packet-Switching Network

INTERACTIVE NETWORKS

Interactive networks allow two-way communication. Providing an interactive service requires that signals travel rapidly to and from the source and the destination of the activity. The telephone network is an example of an interactive network designed to carry voice traffic.

Currently, most residential access to interactive services is through telephone lines, which are generally copper twisted-pair wires that lack the ability to carry interactive video traffic. Consequently, interactive services at the residential level are generally limited to audio and text applications. In contrast, cable television networks carry video traffic into residences using coaxial cable, which has a higher capacity than copper twisted-pair wire. However, the cable networks currently do not have the switching infrastructure needed to provide interactive services to the home.

Fiber-optic cable has higher capacity than either copper twisted-pair or coaxial cable. Although the cost of using fiber-optic cable is decreasing, its cost has historically limited its use to high-traffic trunk routes. More recently, as costs decrease, some telecommunications providers are extending fiber-optic cable from the trunk routes to locations closer to residences. However, extending fiber-optic cable all the way from the trunk routes to individual residences remains costly. Thus, a hybrid coaxial-fiber system will most likely be used to provide residential access to interactive services.

EMERGING TECHNOLOGIES

Several types of telecommunications technologies are emerging that could overcome current technical obstacles or provide new or advanced services. Among these technologies are data compression, techniques of sending audio traffic over a data network, and network enhancements that provide improved or interactive services.

Data compression refers to techniques for compacting digital signals for more efficient transmission or storage. Compressed data can be sent faster, more cheaply, and over lower-capacity networks than can uncompressed data. Data compression is particularly useful for digital video transmission because (1) video normally requires a relatively high network capacity and (2) some data can be lost during compression without significantly affecting the picture's quality. Compression allows, for example, an increase in the number of available residential cable TV channels from 126 to over 500.

Because packet-switched networks are more efficient than circuit-switched networks, some organizations are developing techniques for sending audio traffic over a packet-switched network. One technique, referred to as asynchronous transfer mode (ATM), places digitized audio signals into packets and sends them over a high-speed packet-switched network. The federal government has developed ATM test beds as part of its National Research and Education Network initiative, and several telecommunications firms are now offering commercial ATM technologies Government researchers are investigating very-high-speed networks that challenge the limits of the technology.

Some emerging technologies may provide improved or interactive service over the current telecommunications infrastructure. One such technology called the asymmetrical digital subscriber line, is being tested by the Bell Atlantic telephone company. This technology, if proven successful, will allow video programming to travel over copper twisted-pair telephone lines while allowing concurrent telephone service. Bell Atlantic is testing this technology in northern Virginia. Another example is the implementation of ISDN technology. ISDN is designed to provide interactive telephone and data services simultaneously over a standard copper telephone line. Combined with video compression techniques, ISDN can provide interactive video service over a standard telephone line.

Appendix II

REGULATORS AND BUSINESSES IN THE TELECOMMUNICATIONS INDUSTRY

Regulators have had substantial impact on the telecommunications industry. Regulators seek to promote universal service, ensure markets' stability, protect property rights, promote multiple information sources, and protect consumers from unfair pricing practices. The regulatory structure is administered and influenced through a complex web of state and local governments, FCC, the Congress, the courts, and special interest groups, as figure II.1 indicates. In addition, the telecommunications industry consists of many businesses, each of which is affected in different ways by telecommunications policy.

A NUMBER OF BODIES FORMULATE AND INFLUENCE TELECOMMUNICATIONS POLICY

The following briefly discusses the functions of the entities primarily responsible for formulating telecommunications policy and regulations.

Federal Communications Commission

FCC was established by the 1934 Communications Act as an independent regulatory body responsible for regulating interstate and foreign communication by radio and wire. According to the 1934 act, FCC'S telecommunications policy goal is to make available, as far as possible, to all the people of the United States a rapid, efficient, nationwide, and worldwide wire and radio communication service with adequate facilities at reasonable charges. To achieve this goal, FCC believes it must promote efficiency, universal service, reasonable charges, and innovative services.

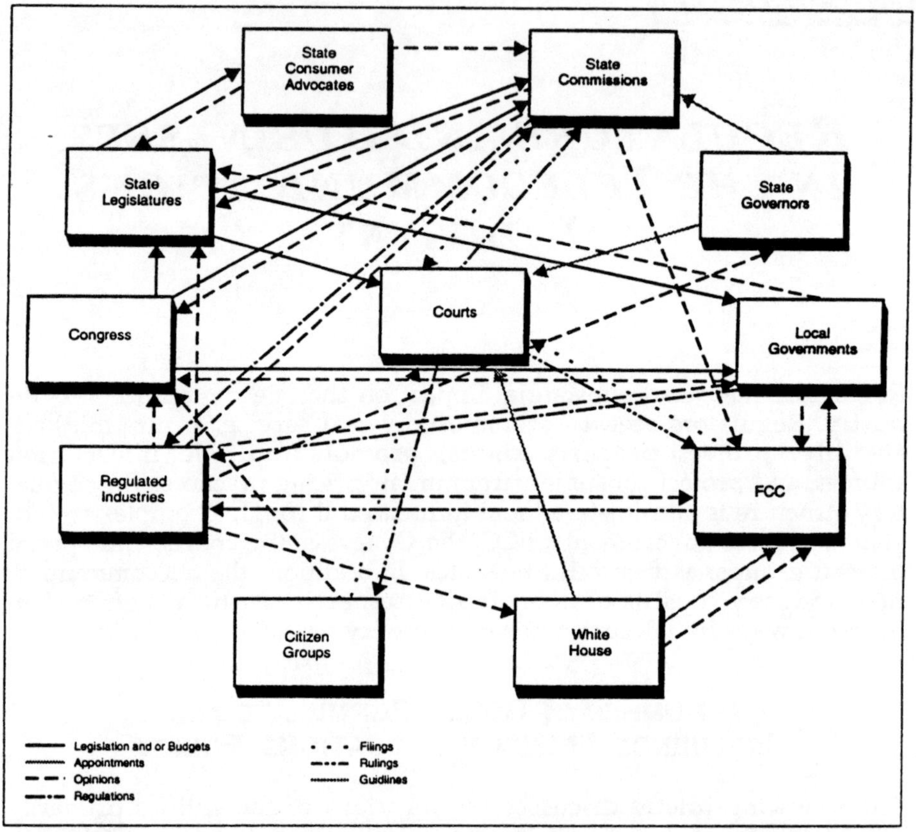

Figure II.1: The arena for formulating telecommunications policy

The Department of Justice

The Department enforces antitrust laws. In 1974, the Department filed suit against AT&T, alleging a number of anticompetitive abuses under the Sherman Antitrust Act. The suit culminated in a consent decree that separated AT&T's long-distance and local telephone service industries. The Department, together with the U.S. district courts, administers the provisions of the consent decree.

The Courts

The federal courts interpret telecommunications legislation and review FCC's actions. The U.S. district court has administered the provisions of the AT&T consent decree, including whether and when the BOCS can begin providing long-distance service, manufacture telecommunications equipment, and provide information services. Pending legislation would shift some of these responsibilities to FCC and the Justice Department.

State and Local Governments

State and local governments generally regulate intrastate telephone services. Among other things, they (1) establish regulatory policies, (2) control the entry of other telephone service providers, and (3) regulate rates.

In addition, a number of organizations exist to assist in formulating public policy and addressing technical issues associated with the Information Superhighway. Examples follow.

Department of Commerce's National Telecommunications and Information Administration

This agency serves as the President's expert adviser on telecommunications matters, including economic and technological advancement and industry regulation. The agency manages the federal government's use of portions of the radio frequency spectrum, coordinate federal telecommunications assistance to state and local governments, a studies and evaluates telecommunications research and development and the impact of the convergence of computer and communications technology.

Interagency Information Infrastructure Task Force

This task force works with the Congress and the private sector to propose the policies and initiatives needed to accelerate the deployment of the Information Superhighway. The task force is chaired by the Secretary of Commerce and includes representatives of the key federal agencies involved in telecommunications and information policy.

Advisory Council on the National Information Infrastructure

The Advisory Council provides advice from the private sector to the Interagency Infrastructure Task Force on (1) the appropriate roles of the private and public sectors in national infrastructure development; (2) the administration's vision for the evolution of the infrastructure; (3) privacy, security, and copyright issues; (4) national strategies for maximizing the interconnection and interoperability of communications networks; and (5) universal access policies. The council is composed of members from industry, labor, academia, public interest groups, and state and local governments.

TELECOMMUNICATIONS INDUSTRY CONSISTS OF MANY PLAYERS

In addition to local and long-distance telephone companies, the telecommunications industry includes a variety of other businesses. Competitive access providers (CAP) compete with local telephone companies for certain types of business in specific locations, while other players include cable, satellite, and broadcast television; cellular and satellite telephone; on-line information services (e.g., Compuserve and Prodigy); and a host of hardware and software manufacturers. Advances in technology have shaped the way these companies have developed and competed. Some companies are in their formative stages, such as direct-broadcast satellite television and satellite telephone services. Others, such as cellular telephone and on-line information services, while established only within the past decade, have achieved substantial growth and now play significant roles in the industry.

Competitive Access Providers

CAPs provide competitive local telephone service alternatives by linking customers to long-distance networks and to other local customers. CAPs currency focus primarily on large-volume customers in major business districts. Many have installed their own fiber-optic infrastructure which facilitates high-capacity services such as videoconferencing. Estimates on the number of CAPs range between 30 and 46. CAPs' customers believe they receive high-quality services, quick response times, and economical prices. However, many states prohibit competition with the local telephone company, and in others, CAPs face franchise fees and other restrictions that do not apply to the local telephone company.

Cable Television Companies

Cable television companies provide a wide variety of programming that is sent to residences mainly over coaxial cable rather than over the air, as in broadcast television. Cable companies retransmit local television broadcast signals and may also offer programs available via satellite transmission, such as C-Span and Cable News Network.

Regulation of the cable television industry has historically involved a mixture of policies, regulations, rules, and procedures administered by federal, state, and local entities. The 1984 Cable Communications Policy Act deregulated the industry. However, in response to continually increasing cable rates, the Congress enacted the Cable Television Consumer Protection and Competition Act of 1992 (commonly known as the 1992 Cable Act), which requires cable rate regulation in areas where effective competition does not exist. FCC estimated that rate reregulation would affect up to three-quarters of the cable systems and cable subscribers across the country.

Personal Communications Services and Cellular Telecommunication Companies

Cellular telephone companies offer mobility for customers when providing local service, some long distance service, and some data services. The cellular industry generally consists of two providers per geographic region and is generally unregulated. Personal Communications Service a lightweight, more portable, and versatile cousin of cellular telephones that is just now emerging—is expected to provide additional data as well as video services. Although FCC allocates spectrum for these industries, they are not generally subject to comprehensive federal and state regulation.

Satellite-Based Services

Satellite television and satellite telephone services can reach rural areas not served by wires. The size and cost of satellite television antennas has been a drawback of this technology. However, two direct-broadcast satellite companies, which will deliver programming to customers using 18-inch dish antennas, are planning to initiate operations in the near future. The companies plan to offer the antennas for about $700 initially but anticipate lower prices as the number of subscriptions increases. In addition, several companies are developing satellite-based telephone systems. The size and cost of this equipment and the expected rates for using the systems present challenges.

Broadcast Companies

Broadcast companies, which provide consumers with the only free radio and television services, are subject to FCC spectrum allocation and content guidelines. Broadcasters believe they are potential participants in the Information Superhighway, since they reach nearly 100 percent of all homes and will soon be able to broadcast data to pagers and fax machines. In addition, broadcasters would like to offer enhanced advertising services. For example, if a viewer desired additional information about an advertised product, the viewer could interactively obtain information on the product's availability or price or perhaps on the location of the nearest dealer.

Digital television is expected to represent the next generation in television technology. Because information in digital format can be compressed into less space than information in analog format, more frequency spectrum is expected to become available when digital television arrives. Broadcasters hope to deliver advanced services over this new-found capacity.

The 1934 Communications Act and certain provisions of the 1984 and 1992 cable acts govern television and radio broadcasters. The 1984 Cable Communications Policy Act prohibits certain types of television-cable cross-ownership. FCC's licenses limit broadcasters' use of allocated spectrum to providing free over-the-air broadcast signals. These rules are intended to ensure multiple ownership and a diverse array of mass media providers. However, broadcasters perceive their regulatory structure as barrier to operating in other lines of businesses.

Electric Utility Companies

Electric utilities plan to use the Information Superhighway's technology and some are considering providing expanded services. Some utilities have been installing fiber-optic cable in their internal communications networks to monitor customers' energy consumption and read meters for billing purposes. These utilities hope to assist customers in managing their demand by suggesting the use of major appliances during off-peak hours. Reduced peak energy demand could postpone the need for utilities to build new power plants. However, because these services use only a portion of the fiber-optic cable's capacity, some utility companies are considering leasing the excess capacity to other communications service providers or possibly providing local telephone service.

Electric utilities are regulated at the state level for intrastate generation, distribution, transmission, and sales by public utility commissions or equivalent agencies and at the federal level for interstate transmissions and wholesale sales by the Federal Energy Regulatory Commission. Existing regulations prevent some of these companies from engaging in non-utility lines of business.

Part B

An Overview of Technology Challenges

ABBREVIATIONS

AIN	advanced intelligent network
ARPA	Advanced Research Projects Agency
AT&T	American Telephone and Telegraph Company
ATM	asynchronous transfer mode
B-ISDN	Broadband Integrated Services Digital Network
BOC	Bell operating company
CAP	competitive access provider
DOD	Department of Defense
FCC	Federal Communications Commission
GEO	geosynchronous Earth orbit
HPCC	High Performance Computing and Communications
Hz	Hertz
IBM	International Business Machines
IDEA	international data encryption algorithm
IITF	Information Infrastructure Task Force
ISDN	Integrated Services Digital Network
Kbps	thousand bits per second
LAN	local area network
LEO	low Earth orbit
Mbps	million bits per second
NANP	North American Numbering Plan
NII	national information infrastructure
NIST	National Institute of Standards and Technology
NSA	National Security Agency
OSI	Office of Special Investigations
PCN	personal communications network
PCS	personal communication system
SAC	service access code
SONET	synchronous optical network
SS7	Signaling System 7
VF	voice frequency
VSAT	very small aperture terminal

Chapter 5

INTRODUCTION

A global technological upheaval, fueld by rapid advances in information processing, storage, switching and transmission technologies, is beginning to blur the lines between computing, telephony, television and publishing. This convergence is creating a new breed of information service industry, and permitting the development of the much discussed National Information Infrastructure (NII), commonly known as the information superhighway. The administration envisions the superhighway as a seamless web of communications networks, computers, databases, and consumer electronics - built, owned, and operated principally by the private sector - that will put vast amounts of information at users' fingertips. It believes that the superhighway, if freed from the constraints imposed by rigid regulatory regimes, will fundamentally change the way we work, learn, shop, communicate, entertain ourselves, and get health care and public services.

Despite the dramatic advances in technology and the changes sweeping the communications industry, the superhighway's development is expected to be slow and arduous. As such, its development should not be viewed as a cliff that is suddenly confronted, but rather an increasingly steep slope that society has been climbing since the early communications networks were established.[1] A national and global information infrastructure, which will serve as the foundation for the superhighway, already exists. Telephones, televisions, radios, computers and fax machines - interconnected through a complex web of fiber optics, wires, cables, satellites, and other communications technologies - are used every day to receive, store, process, display, and transmit data, text, voice, sound, and images in homes and businesses throughout the world. However, the information superhighway is expected to offer much more than separate telephone, data, or video ser-

[1] *What it Takes to Make It Happen: Key Issues for Applications of the National Information Infrastructure,* Committee on Applications and Technology, Information Infrastructure Task Force, January 25, 1994.

vices; it is expected to integrate these services into an advanced high-speed, interactive, broadband, digital communications system.[2]

Some of the advanced capabilities and services envisioned for the superhighway are beginning to be provided - albeit at a relatively high cost and at low transmission speeds - by the existing information infrastructure. For example, the Internet - a global metanetwork, or "network of networks," linking over 59,000 networks, 2.2 million computer systems, and over 15 million users in 92 countries - provides many of the services envisioned for the information superhhighway.[3] Similarly, a growing number of on-line services, such as CompuServe, America Online, and Prodigy, provide their subscribers with a rich array of information services. Finally, hundreds of communities across America are served by electronic bulletin boards dispensing information to hundreds of thousands of users.

The administration, believing that the technologies to create, manipulate, manage, and use information are of strategic importance to the United States, has formed a multiagency group - the Information Infrastructure Task Force (IITF) - to articulate a vision for the information superhighway and to guide its development. The task force, chaired by the Secretary of Commerce, is responsible for addressing a wide range of regulatory and technical issues related to the information superhighway and for the coordination of existing federal efforts in the communications area. The task force is examining, through its committees and working groups, a wide range of technical issues relevant to the development and growth of the information superhighway. A more detailed description of the IITF structure and its activities is presented in Appendix I.

THE GRAND VISION OF THE INFORMATION SUPERHIGHWAY

While industry is beginning to build the information superhighway, little is known about how the superhighway will be structured and what services it will provide. Nevertheless, a common vision of its capabilities is beginning to form among policymakers and public interest

---

[2] In digital networks, analog messages (such as voice) are converted to digital signals (ones and zeroes). Once in digital form, voice, video, graphics, and text can be combined and efficiently stores, compressed, and transmitted. The capacity of a digital network may be descibed in terms of the number of bits that the network can transmit every second. In general, narrowband networks transmit at rates below 1.5 million bits per second (1.5 Mbps); broadband networks transmit at rates above 1.5 Mbps.

[3] Internet users with access to a transmission speed of 56 thousand bits per second (56 Kbps) can receive digital radio or transmit and receive digital files containing embedded text, voice, video and images. However, at current commercial rates, the average fee for attachment to the Internet at 56 Kbps is about $15,000 per year. Users not requiring sophisticated multimedia services may access Internet for about $25 per month.

groups. First, there is an emerging agreement that the superhighway should be structured as a metanetwork that will seamlessly link thousands of broadband digital networks. Second, it should allow a two-way flow of information, with users being able to both receive and transmit large volumes of digital information. Third, it should be open, ensuring equal access for service and network providers. Finally, it should ensure the security and rivacy of databases and users' communications, and provide a high degree of interoperability and reliability.

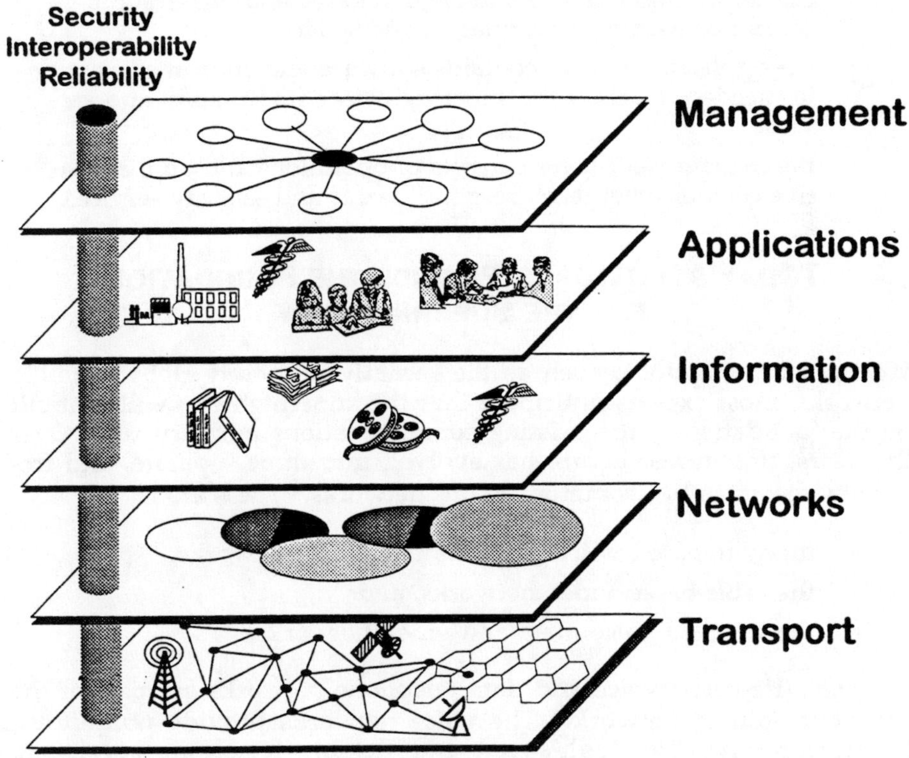

Figure 1.1. Functional layers of the information superhighway

Achieving the grand vision will depend largely on how successfully industry integrates advanced technologies and capabilities into the various layers of the information superhighway. To better understand the integration of advanced telecommunication technologies into the existing communication infrastructure, we developed a conceptual model of the information superhighway, as shown in Figure 1.1.

The model presents the following five critical layers - management, applications, information, networks and transport - linked with pervasive security, interoperability, and reliability requirements.

- the transport layer consists of optical fibers, coaxial cable, copper wire, switches, routers, satellites and transmitters
- the networks layer consists of thousands of logical networks superimposed on the transport layer
- the information layer includes databases and electronic libraries containing text, images, and video
- the applications layer contains software and consumer electronics needed to access the superhighway's information and services
- the management layer consists of operations and administrative centers, emergency response teams and security services.

TODAY'S NETWORKS PROVIDE THE FOUNDATION FOR THE SUPERHIGHWAY

With a few exceptions, such as the recently proposed global satellite networks, most experts anticipate that the superhighway will be built on the foundation of the existing communications infrastructure. Over the years, this infrastructure has evolved into three separate, and frequently incompatible, communications networks.[4] These are

- the wire-based voice and data telephone networks,
- the cable-based video networks, and
- the wireless voice, data and video networks.

The wire-based voice and data telephone networks are part of the global telephone network.[5] The voice networks provide ubiquitous, highly interoperable, high-speed and flexible telephone service to millions of users. The data networks provide high-speed digital data communications services. The cable-based video networks rely on various approaches to broadcast a one-way broadband video signal to individual subscribers. Finally, the wireless networks use a wide range of

---

[4] An additional type of data network - the fiber optic networks used by electric power utilities to manage their power distribution systems - also exists. These networks may eventually become part of the information superhighway.

[5] Unlike the private networks developed for the exclusive use of one organization, the U.S. common carrier netwrks are shared-resource networks that offer communications services to public subscribers.

analog and digital radio technologies to deliver voice, data, and video services.

The principal shortcoming of the existing communications infrastructure is its inability to provide integrated voice, data, and video services. Over the years, the voice and data networks have evolved separately, with voice networks relying on circuit switching while data networks largely using packet switching techniques. Thus, a business user requiring voice, data and videoconferencing services may have to use three separate networks - a voice network, a data network, and a videoconferencing network. The emergence of multimedia applications and the high bandwidth applications in health care, industry, education, and business are beginning to require a network infrastructure capable of supporting multiple types of information.

The basic architecture of the three types of networks is shown in Figure 1.2. (see appendix II for an overview of each of these networks.)

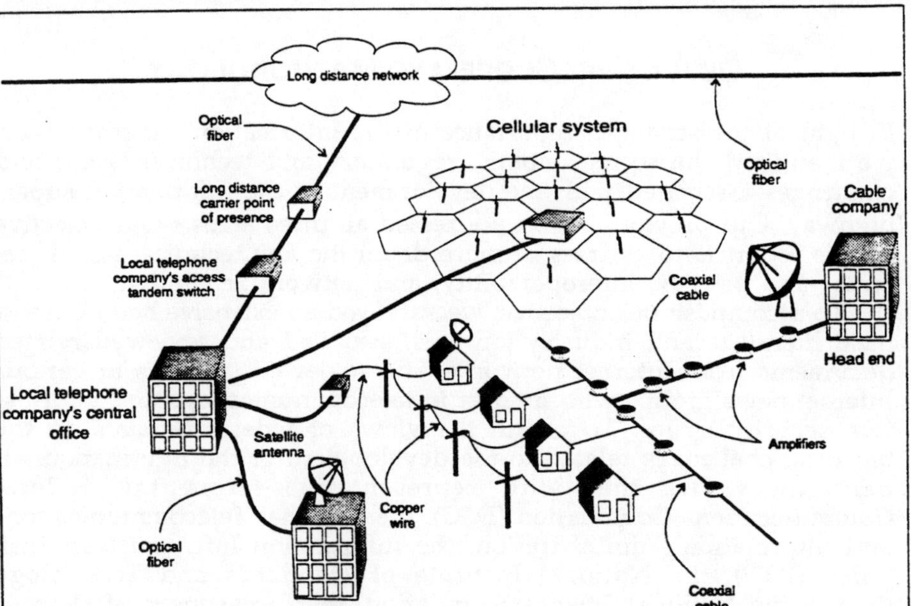

Figure 1.2. Telephone, cable and wireless networks

The communications industry is beginning to introduce several new and innovative technologies that could enable the superhighway's developers to achieve the administration's vision of the information superhighway. These technologies include

- narrowband Integrated Services Digital Network (ISDN),
- advanced signaling and intelligent networks,
- broadened ISDN (B-ISDN),
- personal communications networks, and
- broadband in the local loop.

These technologies, described in more detail in appendix III, will help provide many of the advanced services and capabilities of the information superhighway. The development of the superhighway will also require the expenditure of tens of billions of dollars to build the local broaband "on-ramps" connecting residential, institutional, and business users with the evolving superhighway.[6] Further, its users are expected to be offered viable services and information products beyond the much touted 500 channels of high-definition television.[7]

Objective, Scope and Methodology

In light of the strategic importance of the information superhighway, we identified the socioeconomic, regulatory and technical issues and challenges associated with the development of the information superhighway. Our previous report addressed all three areas.[8] Our objective in this report is to address in more detail the key technical issues: security and privacy, interoperability, and network reliability.

To accomplish our objective, we surveyed an extensive body of technical literature and industry journals, searched and reviewed related documents from Internet networks, and reviewed postings to various Internet news groups with interest in telecommunications and information security issues. To obtain the views of federal officials on the technical challenges related to the development of the information superhighway, we met with representatives from the Federal Communications Commission (FCC), the National Telecommunications and Information Administration, the Information Infrastructure Task Force (IITF), the National Institute of Standards and Technology (NIST), the National Science Foundation, the Department of Defense (DOD), the Advanced Research Projects Agency (ARPA), and the National Security Agency (NSA). We also met with representatives of

---

6 Cable Television Laboratories estimates that the replacement of the copper wire in the local loop will cost hundreds of billions of dollars.

7 Many argue that once the industry provides the on-ramps, a rich array of services requiring interactive, broadband transmission capabilities will be developed. Others believe that the response to the view "if we build it, they will come" is "yes, but will they bring any money?"

8 *Information Superhighway: Issues Affecting Development* (GAO/RCED-94-285, Sept. 30, 1994).

the telephone, cable, and communication industry to obtain their views on technical issues related to the superhighway.

We conducted our work in Washington, D.C. and vicinity between September 1993 and October 1994, in accordance with generally accepted government auditing standards. In addition, we discussed the contents of this report with representatives of the National Telecommunications and Information Administration, IITF, FCC, NIST, DOD, ARPA, and NSA, and have incorporated their comments where appropriate.

Chapter 6

ENSURING SECURITY AND PRIVACY WILL POSE A MAJOR CHALLENGE

Much of the information that will be on the superhighway, including health care records, business documents, engineering drawings, purchase orders, or credit card transactions will be proprietary or privacy sensitive an must be protected. As it evolves, the superhighway will become an increasingly tempting target for intruders with the technical expertise and resources to cause great harm, including insiders,[1] hackers, foreign governments conducting political and military intelligence operations, domestic and foreign enterprises engaged in industrial espionage, and terrorist groups seeking to disrupt our society or cripple our economy.[2] Unauthorized disclosure, theft, modification, or malicious destruction of such information could bankrupt a business, interrupt vital public service, or destroy lives.

Information security plays a key role in protecting computer systems, networks, and information - including voice, fax and data communications - from harm, disclosure or loss. Privacy depends heavily on security.[3] In essence, there is little or no privacy protection afforded by poorly secured information systems and networks. While privacy-enhancing legislation, regulations, and management practices play an

---

1 Many violations of information safeguards are perpetrated by trusted personnel who engage in unauthorized activities or activities that exceed their authority. These insiders may copy, steal, or sabotage information, yet their actions may remain undetected.

2 *Economic Espionage: The Threat to U.S. Industry* (GAO/T-OSI-92-6, Apr. 29, 1992).

3 Privacy is the state of being free from unsanctioned intrusion; a condition in which an individual can determine when, how, and to what extent information about him or her is collected, used and communicated to others.

important role in reducing the threat to individual privacy, it is security technology that will provide many of the safeguards.[4]

Significant effort will be needed to define, develop, test, and implement measures to overcome the security challenge posed by the increasing complexity, interconnectivity, and the sheer size of the evolving superhighway. These measures include identifying the superhighway's security and privacy requirements and developing tools and techniques to satisfy the requirements.

The federal government, because of its extensive experience and expertise in developing secure network, is addressing selected aspects of security and privacy. However, critics of federal involvement argue that the current federal strategy represents a danger to civil liberties and that individuals should be free to choose the technical means for achieving information security. As a result, the challenge will be establishing a reasonable level of consensus among the major players - the government, the computer and communications industry, the business community, and civil liberty groups - on how to ensure information security and privacy on the information superhighway.

Networks and Computer Systems Are Increasingly Vulnerably to Attacks

The vulnerability of interconnected computer systems is periodically highlighted by attacks on the thousands of computer systems connected to the Internet. These attacks provide an important lesson. The Internet - the world's largest network of networks - has many of the same attributes that will eventually be found in the information superhighway. The information superhighway may not only share similar vulnerabilities, but it may face similar, albeit greatly magnified, threats.

Two major security incidents affecting the Internet illustrate the risk to the evolving information infrastructure. On November 8, 1988, thousands of computers connected to the Internet were attacked by a worm.[5] While the worm did not damage or compromise data, it did deny service to thousands of users working at the nation's major research centers. We found that a number of vulnerabilities facilitated this attack, including the lack of a central focal point to address Internet-wide security problems; security weaknesses at host computer sites; and problems in developing, distributing, and installing software

---

4 *Information Security and Privacy in Network Environments,* Office of Technology Assessment, Washington, D.C.: September 1994.

5 Worms are self-contained programs containing malicious code that copy versions of themselves across electronically connected modes.

patches to operating system software.[6] In response to this incident, the Advanced Research Projects Agency established a Computer Emergency Response Team to assist the Internet community in responding to attacks. Several federal agencies and private-sector organizations also established additional computer emergency response teams coordinated by NIST.

Five years later, in January 1994, intruders again exploited similar weaknesses. This time, the attack was more serious. The intruders gained access to a number of hosts (computer systems) linked to the Internet. The intruders then installed software that captured user names, passwords, and hosts' addresses for Internet traffic terminating at, or passing through, the attacked sites. In addition, they installed two Trojan horse programs,[7] one program to provide back-door access for the intruders to retrieve the captured passwords and a second program to disguise the network monitoring process. With this information, the intruders could access 100,000 Internet accounts.[8] The Department of Defense reported that the attacks compromised a major portion of the international commercial networks as well as major portions of the unclassified Defense information infrastructure. Defense functions affected by the attacks included ballistic weapons research, ocean surveillance, and the military health care systems.

Security Measures Are Critical to Minimizing Risk

Reducing the frequency and damage of attacks against the national networks will require a significant effort to provide the tools and resources necessary for the development and deployment of infrastructure-wide security services. These services include

- identification and authentication - the ability to verify a user's identity and a message's authenticity,
- access control and authorization[9] - the protection of information from unauthorized access,
- confidentiality - the protection of information from unauthorized disclosure,

---

[6] *Computer Security: Virus Highlights Need for Improved Internet Management* (GAO/IMTEC-89-57, June 12, 1989).

[7] A Trojan horse is a program that conceals malicious computer code. Typically, a Trojan horse masquerades as a useful program that users would want or need to execute. It performs, or appears to perform, as expected, but also does surreptitious harm.

[8] Computer Incident Advisory Capability team, Department of Energy.

[9] Authorization involves two steps - identification and authentication.

- integrity - the protection of information from unauthorized modification or accidental loss,
- nonrepudiation - the ability to prevent senders from denying they have sent messages and receivers from denying they have received messages, and
- availability - the ability to prevent denial of service, that is, to ensure that service to authorized users is not disrupted.

Cryptography[10] will play a key role in the development of five of the six security services for the information superhighway. It helps, through password encryption, to improve identification and access control; it protects confidentiality and data integrity by encrypting the data; and finally, it improves, through encrypted electronic signature and related means, nonrepudiation services.

Two basic types of cryptographic systems exist: secret key systems (also called symmetric systems) and public key systems (also called asymmetric systems).[11] In secret key cryptography, two or more parties use the same key to encrypt and decrypt data. As the name implies, secret key cryptography relies on keeping the key secret. If this key is compromised, the security offered by cryptography is eliminated. The best known secret key algorithm is the Data Encryption Standard. It is currently the most widely accepted, publicly available symmetric cryptographic algorithm. Secret key systems also require that a secure communications channel be established for the delivery of the secret key from the sender to receiver. Such a secure, nonelectronic communications channel for the distribution of secret keys is costly to establish and maintain.

Unlike secret key cryptography, which employs a single key shared by two or more parties, public key cryptography uses a pair of matched keys for each party. One of these keys is public and the other private. The public key is made known to other parties - mainly through electronic directories - while the private key must be kept confidential. Thus, under the public key system, there is no need to establish a secure channel to distribute keys. The sender encrypts the message with the recipient's freely disclosed, unique public key. The recipient, in turn, uses her unique private key to decrypt the message.

Public key cryptography also enables the user to produce an electronic signature. The user encrypts the signature using the private key, which, when decrypted with the public key, provides verification that the message originated from that user. The best known public key

---

[10] Cryptography is a technique for transforming ordinary text (plaintext) into unintelligible ciphertext through encryption.

[11] A key is a unique sequence of letters, numbers, or combination of both that is used to encrypt and decrypt messages.

algorithm is the Rivest-Shamir-Adelman algorithm.[12] The Pretty Good Privacy software, which implements the Rivest-Shamir-Adelman algorithm, is probably one of the best known public key cryptographic systems.[13] Figure 2.1 highlights the principal features of the secret and public key cryptographic systems.

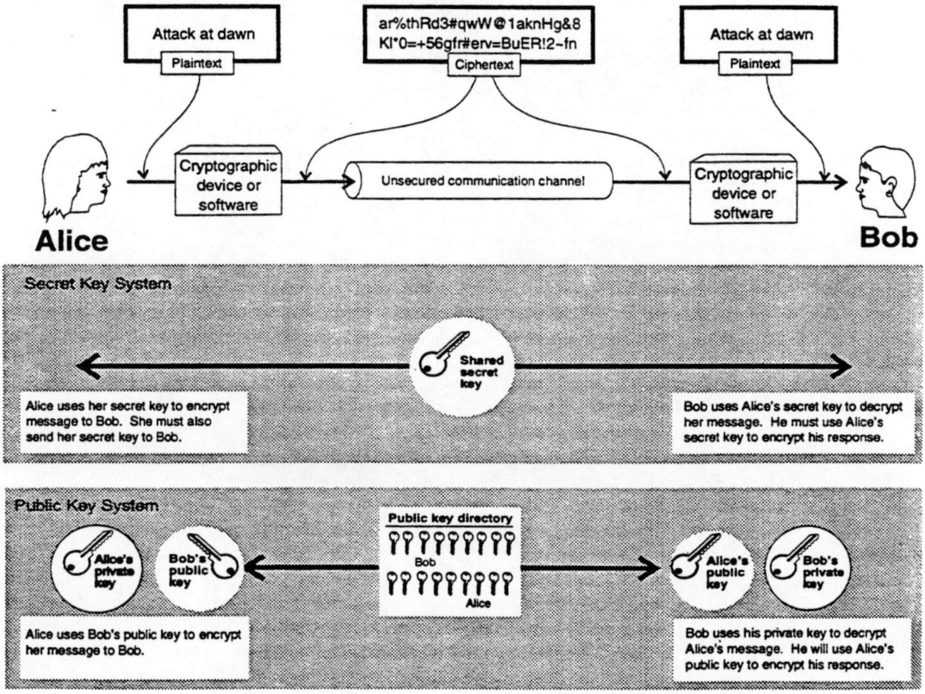

Figure 2.1. Secret and public key encryption systems

A host of related security technologies, including computer memory cards, will also play an important role in securing the information superhighway. Computer memory technology uses a credit-card-size electronic module to store digital information that can be recognized by a network or a host system. Figure 2.2 shows a computer memory card - the Tessera Crypto Card - developed by the National Security

[12] Rivest-Shamir-Adelman is a public key algorithm used for both encryption and authentication; it was invented in 1977 by Ron Rivest, Adi Shamir and Leonard Adelman.

[13] The Pretty Good Privacy is a public key cryptographic system developed by Philip Zimmerman.

Agency.[14] The Tessera Crypto Card is a small portable cryptographic module that provides high-speed authentication and encryption services.

Figure 2.2 Tessera Crypto Card

FEDERAL ROLE IN SECURITY AND PRIVACY IS SUBJECT TO DEBATE

Federal involvement in communication security is fueling a debate over the federal role in regulating the development and use of encryption and communications technologies. Critics of federal involvement, such as the Electronic Frontier Foundation - a public interest organization focused on protecting civil liberties in digital environments - believe that government control of encryption technologies and their implementation represents a danger to civil liberties, and that individuals should be free to choose the technical means for meeting their security requirements. Others, including NIST and Defense officials, maintain that the

14 The Tessera crypto card, based on the Personal Computer Memory Card International Association Industry standard, was recently renamed Fortezza. The card is a key element of the Department of Defense's Multilevel Information Systems Security Initiative.

federal government's participation and guidance in securing the information superhighway may be needed for several reasons. First, the government is a major consumer of telecommunications services and has unique national security and law enforcement needs that must be addressed. Second, the government, and particularly the Department of Defense, has considerable experience in the areas of computer and communications security. Defense, the developer and operator of the world's largest secure communications network, could provide expertise needed to help develop the superhighway's security architecture. The need for such an architecture was underscored by a recent study which noted that it is "imperative to develop at the outset a security architecture that will lay the foundation for protections of privacy, security, and intellectual property rights - safeguards that cannot be supplied as effectively on an add-on basis."[15]

Since the invention of the telegraph and telephone, intelligence and law enforcement agencies have conducted legal intercepts of communications both here and abroad. In general, these agencies used technically simple intercepts that targeted unprotected communications. However, the emergence of digital technologies and the increased availability of sophisticated encryption tools has dramatically eroded the government's electronic intelligence and analysis capabilities. The proliferation of digital communications is making wiretapping increasingly difficult, while robust encryption prevents third parties, including law enforcement and intelligence agencies, from deciphering and understanding intercepted messages.

The administration, after coordination with the Congress, industry and public advocacy groups, has developed a strategy designed to preserve the government's ability to conduct electronic surveillance, wiretapping and analysis of voice and data communications between criminals, terrorists, drug dealers and foreign agents. This strategy includes:

- a major new federal cryptography initiative known as the Key Escrow Standard (popularly known as the "Clipper chip" program),
- the Communications Assistance for Law Enforcement Act requiring the information industry to provide "built-in" wiretapping support in its digital communications systems, and
- restrictions on the export of encryption technology.

15 *Realizing the Information Future*, National Research Council, National Academy Press. Washington, D.C.: 1994, p. 5.

Key Escrow Initiative Intended to Improve Communication Security

The Key Escrow initiative is a voluntary program to improve the security and privacy of telephone communications in the private sector while meeting the legitimate needs of law enforcement. In essence, the initiative is the government's attempt to preempt the threat posed by sophisticated encryption capabilities by offering the industry a relatively inexpensive, albeit government-controlled, hardware-based encryption system capable of providing secure voice, fax and data services. To ensure that law enforcement agencies are able to understand Clipper-encrypted voice communications, the private encryption keys assigned to each individual Clipper chip are to be escrowed with the government. These keys will be made available to law enforcement agencies for court-ordered wire taps.

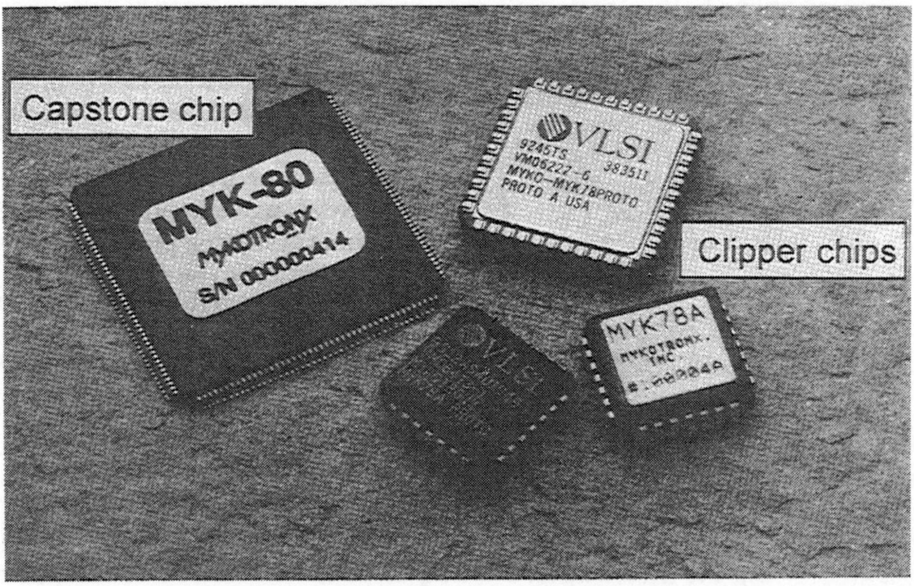

Source: National Security Agency.

Figure 2.3. The Capstone and the Clipper chips.

The Clipper chip, developed by NASA, is a microcircuit incorporating a classified encryption algorithm known as Skipjack.[16] The

[16] The power of the Clipper chip technology is highlighted by comparing it to earlier voice encryption devices. For example, in the early 1940s, the administration asked scientists at the Bell Telephone Laboratories to develop a telephone scrambler that would allow Winston

chip, and its close relative, the Capstone chip, contain a unique key that is used to encrypt and decrypt messages, programmed by the escrow agents.[17] This unique key is then split into two components and delivered to two federal agencies - or escrow agents - for safekeeping. When federal authorities encounter Clipper chip encrypted voice or Capstone chip encrypted data communications during the course of court-authorized wiretapping, they may obtain the unique key necessary for the decryption of the wiretapped communications from the escrow agents. Figure 2.3 shows a Capstone chip and three prototypes of a Clipper chip.

In April 1993, the President directed the Attorney General to (1) request manufacturers of communications hardware that incorporates encryption to install the Clipper chip in their products, and (2) designate two government organizations as "key escrow" holders. The President also directed the Secretary of Commerce to initiate, through NIST, a process to develop federal key escrow encryption standards. Despite strong industry opposition,[18] the administration reaffirmed its 1993 directive and instructed the Secretary of Commerce to approve the Clipper chip as a voluntary national standard for encrypted telephone communications. In February 1994, NIST formally approved the new standard. At the same time, the Attorney General designated NIST and the Automated Systems Design Division of the Department of the Treasury as the key escrow agents.

Critics of the Key Escrow initiative argue that NSA's refusal to declassify and publish the Skipjack encryption algorithm raises the possibility that the algorithm may have a built-in "trap door."[19] Such a trap door would allow intelligence agencies to decrypt Clipper and Capstone encrypted communications at will, without obtaining the private keys from the escrow agents.[20] The critics also note that since robust encryption technology is available both in the U.S. and abroad,

---

Churchill and President Roosevelt to have secure conversations. Code named "Sigsaly," this transatlantic scrambler needed, at the London end, not only a five foot height intermediate scrambler cabinet, but also over 30 seven foot tall relay racks weighting eighty tons, 72 different radio frequencies, a large air-conditioned room, and 30 kW of energy to encipher one short conversation (*The Cabinet War Rooms*, Imperial War Museum, London, 1994).

[17] The Clipper chip is designed to encrypt voice transmissions; the Capstone chip is designed to encrypt data and video transmission.

[18] In July 1993, NIST asked industry to comment on the proposed standard. Of the 320 respondents, only 2 supported the proposed standard.

[19] A trap door is a hidden software or hardware mechanism that allows systems controls to be circumvented. Software developers often introduce trap doors in their code to enable them to reenter the system later and perform certain functions.

[20] On more than one occasion, administration officials, including the Deputy Director of NIST, have testified before Congress that the Skipjack algorithm does not incorporate a trap door mechanism.

there is no incentive for domestic and international industry or private citizens to adopt the Clipper/Capstone technology.

The misgivings about the Key Escrow initiative were also shared by the Computer System Security and Privacy Advisory Board.[21] In its June 4, 1993, resolution, the Board stated that the administration has not (1) provided a convincing a statement of the problem that Clipper attempts to solve, (2) considered other escrow alternatives including the designation of a third, non-government escrow agent, and (3) fully examined the legal and economic implications of the Clipper chip initiative. The Board recommended that the Key Escrow encryption technology not be deployed beyond current implementations planned within the Executive Branch until the significant public policy and technical issues inherent with this encryption technique are fully understood. The Congress asked the National Research Council to conduct a comprehensive study of national cryptography policy and submit, within 2 years, a report to the Secretary of Defense.[22] In December 1993, the Board endorsed the proposal, noting that the study should be conducted as quickly as possible.

In July 1994, the administration reaffirmed its commitment to the Key Escrow scheme in general, and to the use of the Clipper chip for telephone communications in particular. It also offered a compromise on the development of the Capstone chip for computer and video networks. Specifically, the administration said that it understood the concerns that industry has regarding the Capstone chip and welcomed the opportunity to work with industry to design a more versatile, less expensive system. NIST and the information security industry have not initiated a joint effort to explore alternative approaches. Such alternative key escrow schemes would be implemented in software, firmware, or hardware, or a combination thereof; would not rely on a classified algorithm; would be voluntary, and would be exportable.[23]

Legislation Enacted to Facilitate Digital Wiretaps

To address concerns about the potential loss of wiretapping capability due to the rapid deployment of digital communications,[24] in October

---

21 The Board, composed of representatives from the computer and telecommunications industry, independent experts in telecommunications, and federal employees, was established by the Computer Security Act of 1987 to advise the Secretary of Commerce and the Director of NIST on security and privacy issues.

22 Public Law 103-160, Section 267.

23 Letter from Vice President Al Gore to the Honorable Maria Cantwell, House of Representatives, July 20, 1994.

24 *Electronic Surveillance: Technologies Continue to Pose Challenges* (GAO/T-AIMD-94-173, Aug. 11, 1994).

1994 the Congress enacted the Communications Assistance for Law Enforcement Act.[25] The act requires common carriers to ensure that they posses sufficient capability and capacity to accommodate law enforcement's wiretaping needs. Specifically, the act requires that telecommunications carriers develop the capability to expeditiously isolate the content and call-identifying information of a targeted communication and enable the government to access targeted communication at a point away from the carrier's premise. The act requires the government to reimburse carriers for all reasonable costs associated with complying with the act's requirements. Critics of the act - including the Electronic Frontier Foundation - argue that it further erodes communication privacy, and that the Federal Bureau of Investigation has not adequately documented its need for sophisticated digital wiretap capability.

Federal Government Restricts the Export of Encryption Technology

Many of the U.S. encryption technologies, whether developed commercially or by the government, are subject to export controls. The Departments of State and Commerce share responsibility for controlling the exports of these technologies.[26] However, computer industry representatives view the encryption export controls as counterproductive and economically damaging. For example, the representatives noted that because robust, sophisticated encryption technologies, including technologies on the U.S. Munitions List, are widely available in foreign markets, the export controls are reducing their international sales.[27]

Our brief search of foreign Internet sites confirms industry's assertion that sophisticated encryption software is widely available to foreign users. For example, we found that a number of European Internet sites are offering U.S.-made encryption software. In less than two hours, we identified several European sites offering the Pretty Good Privacy software, obtained it from an Internet site in Great Britain, installed the software on our computer, and encrypted a message (shown in Figure 2.4).

---

25 Public Law 103-414.

26 Certain encryption products are placed on the U.S. Munitions List. These products require a munitions license for export to foreign countries.

27 *Communications Privacy: Federal Policy and Actions*, (GAO/OSI-04-2, Nov. 4, 1993).

Plaintext Message With Encrypted Signature

—BEGIN PGP SIGNED MESSAGE—

Our brief search of foreign Internet sites confirms industry's assertion that sophisticated encrytpion software is widely available to foreign users.

—BEGIN PGP SIGNATURE—
Version: 2.6

iQCVAgUBLkEE7iR4seyvySXFAQGqJAQAmTge8TslZTiXIt4cgrBr6qG
ZZfMkEvIm IVFVMP41xWlME+uzJiKWIydWUpXHFi0EzR337I3Nx54N
JyoSoHE1zuAuLR0sVq+7 QMNFaHby2s0HAgByUH6SEHAyCyQZ1UB
m+8Unrb2tsgfNIf6nQfW6z0F4TUV5QNpL bXQiU6JuyEI=
=ErFY

—END PGP SIGNATURE—

Encrypted Message

—BEGIN PGP MESSAGE—
Version: 2.6

hIwCZXmEuMepZt0BBACl0wb3FtNerMXZlAPAVWkaVP9tes44j98sJREVwg
COMLFr IIhvJrm7KA1wiGdHTQXLvdyJNm3PHAXZqKz31eA/WeJRO/cFf1jT
Hx0cCg5Q/buY SdewGCl8gqGG6TyQujBPw73qz93uUSA3/jpzhjI3EiE9sSaK
i6Qjd1KV14o1nYSM AiR4seyvySXFAQP9Gogj63PMFnYiHSV8pPk7tUcwjp
FNXan6pVViwt6JowSbPtUP ib4p6XfI6D0ZjzhlJ9Jwd4A9jpD91tRn5kUnz2D
YNS1ZtJIasWYUMTBYy/lm/QMC 7qaIFKpqjVMOBkiy9Tbz3ToShS7ae2ac
OnWovJkjBjP70CfGJLo0AsEz+1mmAAAB Th/6nhH7IAN+9cQ7gEfl0jJKuK/
uRdVHemACEBLBbIqK2ELog+9hMfRA4eV4vROK 0I9A2wEMQg4DPORS
wrUVQlyehGPQok86EMI1fG0t7bH/SjrdAg/zS1HbwtaWQM51 g9+sfFCiktD
kaETdUZjs+zCPhlS5jy6MpOcvt9x3hkwv50iHpOtfjZ3zHUml3827 +SCJJOA
x4aZ50blBoeEQJHC0/NPPb++A0cCNS5rvktvgG/jFN1porVHex/3301DY dni
hIcs0r33nWAhCG1jIH6hiufUvoXKxpSWX+KUXROS1HZYo84/541g2O6pfk
dQO 3l0yJZlJRL9xPp0nfZC6MaHEGPnMZRqoF3gB7xbU5PUUOrkXIMoq8
tzVOxmAJpwq R9DKkWht356VRVBjkFlQ9pIZTuQ/JBcToWrgk56i/xTWldcb
ks4S75dbreYB1sM= =YCVl

—END PGP MESSAGE—

Figure 2.4. Message encrypted with the Pretty Good Privacy encryption system.

Chapter 7

ACHIEVING INTEROPERABILITY IS A CRITICAL GOAL

Interoperability - the ability of two or more components of a system or network to interact with each other in a meaningful way - is a key goal of the information superhighway. However, full interoperability among the thousands of networks, communications devices, and services that will comprise the information superhighway will be difficult to achieve. To do so, governments, industry, and standards-setting organizations must agree on well-defined international standards for rapidly advancing communications technologies, while manufacturers and service providers need to provide products and services conforming to these standards. However, the telecommunications industry is already deploying, or plans to deploy, a host of technologies and services that are based on ill-defined, anticipatory, or competing standards. To address this dilemma, the federal and private sectors have initiated interoperability efforts, including the assessment of various "open network" architectures.[1]

INTEROPERABILITY WILL BE DIFFICULT TO ACHIEVE

Interoperability will define the information superhighway. Without interoperability, the information superhighway will be fragmented into thousands of poorly integrated communications networks providing a bewildering choice of incompatible services. While policy makers public interest groups, and industry agree that interoperability is a key requirement, they also agree that it will be difficult to achieve among the thousands of communications networks, computers, databases, and consumer electronics that will comprise the information superhighway.

1 The National Research Council defines an open network as one that is capable of carrying information services of all kinds, from suppliers to customers, across network service providers of all kinds, in a seamless, accessible fashion.

As discussed in chapter 1, the existing infrastructure suffers from significant interoperability problems.

New Technologies Being Deployed are Based on Ill-Defined, Anticipatory, and Competing Standards

Because of competitive pressures, the desire to provide new capabilities, and a belief that the traditional standards-setting process is unable to keep up with the fast pace of technological change industry is deploying, or is planning to deploy, a host of new technologies and services. However, many of these technologies and services are based on ill-defined, anticipatory, or competing standards, thereby further complicating efforts to achieve interoperability.

The effects of deploying new technology based on ill-defined standards is illustrated by the implementation of the ISDN. ISDN is an end-to-end digital network evolving from the existing telephone network. It is viewed as the first step in the conversion to a fully digital network. However, the initial deployment of ISDN resulted in the proliferation of "island" ISDN services that could not interoperate because the ISDN standards provided only a broad outline and lacked enough detail to ensure that all implementations would be identical. For example, ISDN users in New York and New England are unable to communicate data with ISDN users in the middle atlantic states. To alleviate the ISDN interoperability problems, the industry announced a plan to establish a consistent interface that would provide interoperability between local telephone companies, long distance telephone companies, and equipment manufacturers.

The deployment of the Asynchronous Transfer Mode (ATM) services provides an example of a technology deployed based on anticipatory standards. The broadband ISDN (B-ISDN) technology, which is expected to lay the foundation for the superhighway's interactive, high-speed digital communications infrastructure, will rely on ATM/SONET optical fiber networks.[2] However, critical ATM standards including global routing and addressing, resource management, multicast,[3] and network management remain undefined. The industry is also developing products and services in the absence of less visible, but equally important standards, for data display and exchange, accounting and billing, network addressing and naming, and telephone number portability (see Appendix IV).

---

[2] ATM is a fast packet switching technology utilizing small, fixed-size cells. Synchronous Optical Network (SONET) is the U.S. implementation of an international synchronous digital hierarchy standard for optical carrier networks.

[3] Multicast is a variant of broadcast, where information can be sent to selected recipients instead of all subscribers of a particular communications systems.

The introduction of competing technologies is highlighted by the deployment of digital cellular systems. Digital cellular systems are viewed as a key component of the evolving personal communications networks. While digital systems will offer dramatically better performance than their analog counterparts, their near-term value in serving as a key link in the emerging B-ISDN network is reduced by compatibility problems. There are three principal digital cellular standards - the U.S. standard, known as the North American Dual-Mode Cellular System; the European standard known as Global System for Mobile Communications; and the Japanese Digital Cellular standard. Although all three standards are based on the time division multiple mode access technique,[4] they are not interoperable.

The Federal and Private Sectors Have Initiated Efforts to Address Interoperability

While the key players - the federal government, the computer and communication industries, and various user groups - appear to agree on the need for a fully interoperable information superhighway, there is no agreement yet on how it should be achieved. The principal federal organizations focused on superhighway interoperability include NIST and the National Research Council's Computer Science and Telecommunications Board.[5] The overall coordination of federal interoperability efforts is being examined by IITF's Technology Policy Working Group. In the private sector, the FCC is working with industry to ensure the interoperability of selected technologies deployed in public networks. Industry has also established a consortium for the development and testing of superhighway applications.

National Research Council Advocates High-Level Architecture to Guide Interoperability Efforts

One promising approach to the planning for interoperability is to develop a high-level architecture - or framework - of the superhighway. This approach was advocated by a recent National Research Council report that presented a vision of the superhighway based on an open data network concept. [6] Under this concept, the superhighway must be

---

4 A digital encoding scheme that allows users to simultaneously transmit on the same frequency by allocating each user a discrete time slot.

5 The federal interagency High Performance Computing and Communications program is also addressing a wide range of network interoperability issues.

6 *Realizing the Information Future,* National Research Council, National Academy Press, Washington, D.C.: 1994.

- open to users: it does not force users into closed groups or deny access to any sector of society, but permits universal connectivity, as does the telephone system,
- open to service providers: it provides an open and accessible environment for competing commercial or intellectual interests, including information providers,
- open to network providers: it makes it possible for any network providers to meet the necessary requirements to attach and become a part of the aggregate of interconnected networks, and
- open to change: it permits the introduction of new applications and services over time; it also permits the introduction of new transmission, switching, and control technologies as these become available.

This concept, expressed as a high-level network architecture, could provide a set of specifications to guide the detailed design of the information superhighway. Without such a framework, the pieces of the emerging superhighway may not fit together. The IITF's Technology Policy Working Group is planning to examine the open data network concept and its applicability to various industries, including cable television, broadcasting, communications and computer.

Industry Responds to Interoperability Problems

In an attempt to improve interoperability, the Network Operations Forum of the Alliance for Telecommunications Industry Solutions established the Internetwork Interoperability Test Plan Ad Hoc Committee. However, the committee's effort was limited to solving problems with the Signaling System 7 (SS7)[7] switching systems. The requirements for intranetwork, product-to-product, and stand-alone equipment modeling and testing were considered to be outside of the committee's charter. Other aspects of existing networks such as interoperability testing requirements of newer technologies were also not addressed. So far, the committee has developed scenarios designed to test the interoperability of SS7 systems.

[7] SS7 is an international common-channel signaling system.

Chapter 8

NETWORK RELIABILITY IS EMERGING AS A KEY CHALLENGE

Ensuring the reliability[1] of the information superhighway will be essential. The public and private sectors are increasingly dependent on the existing telecommunications networks, which will be the foundation of the information superhighway, to meet their business needs. Yet recent outages on these networks have raised concerns and caused economic losses. Moreover, new technologies and industry trends will likely increase network vulnerability, making reliability of the superhighway a key challenge. The government and industry have recently taken several steps to address reliability, including the formation of the Network Reliability Council and the Alliance for Telecommunications Industry Solutions.

RELIABILITY OF THE SUPERHIGHWAY WILL BE ESSENTIAL

In providing critical commercial and personal services, the superhighway will require a highly reliable network. The nation is already dependent on the existing networks, which will provide the underpinning for the superhighway. For example, in addition to conventional telephone services, computers are networked together, facsimile machines provide almost instant access to images and documents, and teleconferencing and videoconferencing have emerged as substitutes for travel. The number of electronic transactions conducted over these networks is enormous. For example, the value of the telephone transactions that take place daily on Wall Street exceeds one trillion dollars. Similarly, the Federal Aviation Administration relies on the public

---

1 Reliability is the probability that a system will not fall over a given period of time and under specified conditions. It is based on the combined reliability of all the components that make up the system, their interconnections, and the environment in which the system operates.

network to transmit air traffic control information between individual airports.

Public telephone networks are also being increasingly relied upon for emergency services. For example, the telephone has replaced fire alarm boxes as the primary method for reporting fires. Emergency 911 service can be obtained from personal or public pay phones. Telephones are also used to report medical emergencies requiring emergency medical technicians, burglaries and domestic problems requiring responses from the police. Enhanced 911 service, available in many locations, is even capable of automatically routing the emergency call to a public service answering point, the facility in charge of answering calls and dispatching appropriate services in the caller's area. The system also searches phone company databases to determine and report the caller's location and telephone number to the dispatcher.

Recent Network Outages Have Raised Concerns and Caused Economic Losses

While the public and private sectors are becoming more dependent on networks, a growing number of major outages have raised concerns, triggered losses of service, potentially risked lives, and affected the economy. Several of these outages are highlighted below.

May 8, 1988: More than 500,000 business and residential customers lost telephone service due to a fire at the Hinsdale, Illinois, central office. During the following two weeks, approximately 3.5 million calls were disrupted. Hospitals with centrex service in the affected area could not make calls from one floor to another. Twenty percent of the departing flights from O'Hare International Airport were canceled and flights from other airports around the country had to be rescheduled. In a study of the Hinsdale outage, the University of Minnesota concluded that the cost of network failures to airlines could be between $2 and $3 million per hour and investment bankers could lose up to $5 million per hour.

Jan. 4, 1991: Maintenance workers in a cable vault in New Jersey accidentally cut an optical fiber transmission line that provided service to lower Manhattan. Sixty percent of the calls into and out of the city were disrupted for eight hours. The New York Mercantile Exchange and the Commodity Exchange had to shut down operations. Voice and radar systems that are used to control air traffic from facilities in New York, Washington, and Boston were disabled for five hours.

Sept. 17, 1991: Through a power sharing arrangement with New York's Consolidated Edison, AT&T agreed to use its own power when Consolidated Edison's facilities were heavily loaded.[2] On this particularly warm day in September, AT&T switched to its own power. Batteries designed to meet the initial instantaneous power demand performed as intended. However, alarms that were intended to inform technicians to start the facility's diesel generator had been manually disabled. When the batteries is charged, all telephone transmission systems in the facility failed. Voice and data communications between the New York, Boston, and Washington Air Route Traffic Control Centers stopped. Three New York area airports closed for several hours. Flights destined for New York were either delayed or canceled. Air traffic at Boston was severely disrupted and delays occurred nationwide. More than 1,174 flights were canceled or delayed and approximately 85,000 passengers were affected. The day after the phone outage, flight schedules were still disrupted because aircraft were not at the right airports for the scheduled morning flights.

Sept. 10, 1993: A road crew boring holes for highway road signs in Ohio cut a high-capacity fiber-optic cable belonging to MCI.[3] The cable which carries most of the company's east-to-west traffic, was repaired in about seven hours. However, millions of residential and business customers were unable to make coast-to-coast calls during that period.

March 15, 1994: During the early morning hours a fire broke out in Pacific Bel's Los Angeles central office known as the Madison Complex. Before complete service was restored, almost 17 hours later, approximately 395,000 customers may have been affected and over 5 million calls were blocked.

Cable cuts, a source of major outages, occurred 160 times during the period between March 1, 1992, and February 4, 1993, with 93 (58 percent) of them caused by "dig-up" incidents, such as the one illustrated in figure 4.1. The average time needed to restore service after a cable cut was 5.2 hours with a maximum of 21.4 hours. The average time required to repair a fiber cable cut was 14.2 hours with a maximum of 97.5 hours.

---

2 Wall Street Journal, December 12, 1991.

3 Wall Street Journal, September 13, 1993.

Source: AT&T Technology Magazine.

Figure 4.1. Fiber optic cable "dig-up" accident.

On February 13, 1992, the FCC instituted mandatory outage reporting requirements for outages that affect more than 30,000 customers for durations lasting 30 minutes or longer. As of June 1994, more than 314 outages were reported. The calculation of the cost of an outage is difficult because of the variety of users that could be affected.

New Technologies, Network Growth, and Complexity Will Likely Increase Network Vulnerability

The deployment of advanced technologies, such as intelligent network architectures, common channel signaling, integrated services digital network, broadband transport facilities, customer control, and user-programmability, is increasing network complexity and vulnerability. The new technologies, described in appendix II, are also allowing network designers to concentrate more traffic into larger and fewer switches, and to rely on fewer higher capacity fiber optic cables to transmit hundreds of thousands of telephone calls. Failure of any of these high-capacity elements could be potentially devastating.

As the information superhighway grows, the number of networks and service providers is also expected to grow. Telecommunications consumers will increasingly acquire services from combinations of suppliers' products, service providers, and network providers. Increasing network complexity will make it more difficult to isolate and correct problems.

The Government and Industry Are Taking Steps to Address Reliability

In 1991, the FCC, concerned about the spate of telephone network outages that affected a large number of subscribers on both the east and west coasts, established the Network Reliability Council. The council's goal was to bring together leaders of the telecommunications industry, telecommunications experts from academia, and consumer organizations, to explore and recommend measures that would enhance network reliability. Members include the executive officers of most of the major U.S. telephone companies, principal equipment suppliers, long-distance companies, consumer organizations, corporate and federal user representatives, and state regulatory agencies.

The council established a steering committee and seven focus groups to deal with the key problem areas - signaling network systems, digital cross-connect systems, fiber cable cuts, fire prevention, enhanced 911 service, power systems, and switching systems (with a focus on software). The groups formulated recommendations for developing and implementing countermeasures to reduce the number of outages; monitoring the results; and modifying, as necessary, the countermeasures. The commission is now looking at these recommendations and considering regulations that would require the carriers and equipment suppliers to implement them.

In 1994, the Network Reliability Council restructured and created four focus groups. The first group will concentrate on network reliability; the second will examine reliability issues arising from expanded interconnection of networks; the third will study network technology and examine reliability concerns related to providing telephone service through cable, satellites and wireless systems; and the fourth group will study the reliability of critical services, including 911, Federal Aviation Administration, military and government.

The Alliance for Telecommunications Industry Solutions - a private sector organization - was formed to promote the timely establishment of telecommunications standards and operational guidelines. Its members include representatives of local exchange carriers, interexchange carriers, enhanced service providers, manufacturers, vendors, and end users who participate in a number of sponsored committees.

The alliance also sponsors the Network Operations Forum, a group of telecommunications industry access providers and customers who meet periodically to identify national operations issues involving the installation, testing, and maintenance of access services. In July 1991, the alliance began focusing on the area of network reliability. One of the forum's subcommittees has developed traffic management guidelines that provide network management personnel with alternatives when emergencies occur. The forum also maintains contact directories for use in emergency situations.

Chapter 9

CONCLUSIONS

While the information superhighway's development is expected to be arduous, a grand vision of its capabilities is beginning to emerge among policy makers, industry leaders, and public interest groups. Viewed as a global metanetwork that will seamlessly and reliably link millions of users through broadband terrestrial and satellite digital networks, it is hoped that the superhighway will allow users to routinely receive and transmit large volumes of digital information, and ensure equal access for service and network providers. Achieving the grand vision will depend largely on how successfully industry and government meet the key technical challenges of security and privacy, interoperability, and reliability.

Security and privacy of databases and users' communications is a critical issue. The superhighway will become an increasingly enticing target for intruders with the technical expertise and resources to cause damage. Given the complexity, size, and importance of the evolving superhighway, significant effort will be needed to define, develop, test and implement security measures.

Interoperability among the thousands of networks, communications devices, and services that will comprise the superhighway is also essential, but will be difficult to achieve. The telecommunications industry is deploying, or plans to deploy, a host of technologies and services that are based on ill-defined, anticipatory, or competing standards. A coordinated approach will help reduce the risk of the superhighway being fragmented into thousands of poorly integrated networks providing a bewildering choice of incompatible services.

Because the proposed superhighway is intended to provide critical commercial and personal services, its end-to-end reliability requirements will be very high. The public and private sectors are already highly dependent on the existing telecommunications infrastructure and networks that will be the foundation of the superhighway. Outages on these networks have raised concerns about achieving reliability.

Government and industry are beginning to recognize these challenges. The administration's Information Infrastructure Task Force, working together with the private sector, has formed committees and working groups charged with addressing security and privacy, interoperability, and reliability issues. The challenge remains for the major public and private players to work together to resolve these issues. With effective cooperation, the promise of the information superhighway can be attained.

Appendix I

INFORMATION INFRASTRUCTURE TASK FORCE IS ADDRESSING SELECTED TECHNICAL ISSUES

The administration formed the Information Infrastructure Task Force (IITF) to articulate and implement its vision for the information superhighway. The task force includes high-level representatives of federal agencies that play a major role in the development and application of information and telecommunications technologies. Working together with the private sector, the participating agencies plan to develop comprehensive technology, telecommunications, and information policies and promote applications that best meet the needs of both the agencies and the country. By helping build consensus on difficult policy issues, the IITF is planning to enable agencies to make and implement policy more quickly and effectively.

The Secretary of Commerce chairs the IITF, and much of the staff work and administrative support for the task force is being done by Commerce's National Telecommunications and Information Administration. The task force operates under the aegis of the White House Office of Science and Technology Policy and the National Economic Council. The administration has also established the United States Advisory Council on the National Information Infrastructure to facilitate private sector input to the IITF. The Secretary appointed 37 members to serve a two-year term on the advisory council. The council members represent the many different stakeholders in the information superhighway, including industry, labor, academic, public interest groups, and state and local governments.

The task force is undertaking a wide-ranging examination of all issues relevant to the development and growth of the information superhighway. The Administration's Agenda for Action, released September 15, 1993, identified nine specified principles and goals to guide government action:

- promoting private sector investment,
- extending the "universal service" concept to ensure that information resources are available to all at affordable prices,
- promoting technological innovation and new applications,
- promoting seamless and interactive operation,
- ensuring information security and network reliability,
- improving management of the radio frequency spectrum,
- protecting intellectual property rights,
- coordinating with other levels of government and with other nations, and
- providing access to government information and improving government procurement.

To carry out its responsibilities, the IITF established three committees - Telecommunications Policy, Information Policy, and Applications and Technology. The Telecommunications Policy Committee is responsible for formulating a consistent administration position on key telecommunications issues. The committee has established the following four working groups.

- The universal service working group works to ensure that all Americans have access to and can enjoy the benefits of the information superhighway.
- The network reliability and vulnerability working group works to (1) ensure that the superhighway will provide protection for all users from catastrophic failure of the network, along with mechanisms for recovery from threats ranging from natural disasters to overt attacks; and (2) define and monitor national security and emergency preparedness requirements.
- The international telecommunications working group examines international telecommunications issues. This working group is subdivided into five subworking groups that are addressing:

    - the participation of foreign governments/foreign corporations in the superhighway and the use of the superhighway to open overseas markets,
    - the effects of current law on setting policy, and legislative efforts to change the law,
    - the federal government's controls of technology exports,
    - U.S. participation in international organizations and standards-setting bodies, and

- The legislative drafting task force is to formulate the administration's telecommunications legislative reform initiatives.

The Information Policy Committee has five working groups that are addressing critical information policy issues:

- The intellectual property rights working group is to develop proposals for protecting copyrights and other intellectual property rights in an electronic world.
- The privacy working group is to develop proposals to protect individual privacy.
- The government information working group is to focus on ways to promote dissemination of government data in electronic form.
- The Freedom of Information Act legislation working group is to define public access rights to government electronic records.
- The scientific and technical information group is to focus on ways to manage technical and scientific information.

The Committee on Applications and Technology coordinates the administration's efforts to develop, demonstrate, and promote applications of information technology in manufacturing, education, health care, government services, libraries, environmental monitoring, electronic commerce and other applications. It has three working groups:

- The government information technology services working group coordinates efforts to improve the application of information technology by federal agencies.
- The technology policy working group addresses cross-cutting technology issues related to interoperability and scalability of new telecommunications and information services.
- The health information and applications working group coordinates efforts that affect use of the superhighway for health care.

The IITF has also established the NII Security Issues Forum to coordinate security efforts across the committees and working groups of the IITF.

Appendix II

DESCRIPTION OF EXISTING NETWORK TECHNOLOGIES

The following provides a brief overview of the three major types of communication networks that comprise the existing communication infrastructure - the wire-based voice and data telephone networks; the cable-based video networks; and the wireless, voice, data, and video networks.

THE TELEPHONE NETWORKS

The telephone system is the world's largest switched distributed network providing point-to-point voice, fax, data, and videoconferencing services to hundreds of millions of subscribers. It is also, at first glance, the primary foundation for the information superhighway. It is ubiquitous, highly interoperable, and reliable. It is capable of handling millions of simultaneous calls, and it provides accurate usage tracking and billing. In the U.S., voice, data, and videoconferencing services are provided by the local exchange carriers (local telephone companies) serving the local access and transport areas, and by the interexchange carriers (long distance carriers) providing long distance and international dialing services through their long distance networks.[1] Although the industry is rapidly introducing advanced digital communication technologies, the telephone network continues to be dependent on analog transmission.[2]

---

[1] The local telephone companies, created in the wake of the breakup of AT&T, include 22 Bell Operating Companies organized into seven regional Bell holding companies - Pacific Telesis, US West, Ameritech, Southwestern Bell, BellSouth, Bell Atlantic, and NYNEX. Many local area and transport areas are also served by independent telephone companies. The major long distance carriers include AT&T, MCI, U.S. Spring, Advanced Telecommunications Corporation and Wiltel.

[2] During the 1980's, the telephone service providers replaced most of their older electromechanical switches with analog or digital computer-driven switches.

Much of today's telephone service is based on two analog-oriented transmission technologies - the analog voice frequency (VF) systems and the digital T-carrier system. The VF system supports voice transmission over a pair of copper wires - also known as the local loop - connecting millions of residential and business subscribers with the local telephone company's central offices. The T-carrier system plays a major role in the first step in the transition from analog to digital capabilities. One of the fastest growing segments of services offered by the local telephone companies and the long distance carriers, the system can provide transmission speeds up to 274.176 Mbps. The basic building block of the T-carrier technology is a single VF voice channel digitized into a 64 Kbps data stream; a T-1 line carries 24 digitized voice channels, an aggregate of 1.544 Mbps. The T-carrier digital hierarchy allows T-1 lines to be combined to provide transmission rates of up to 274.176 Mbps.

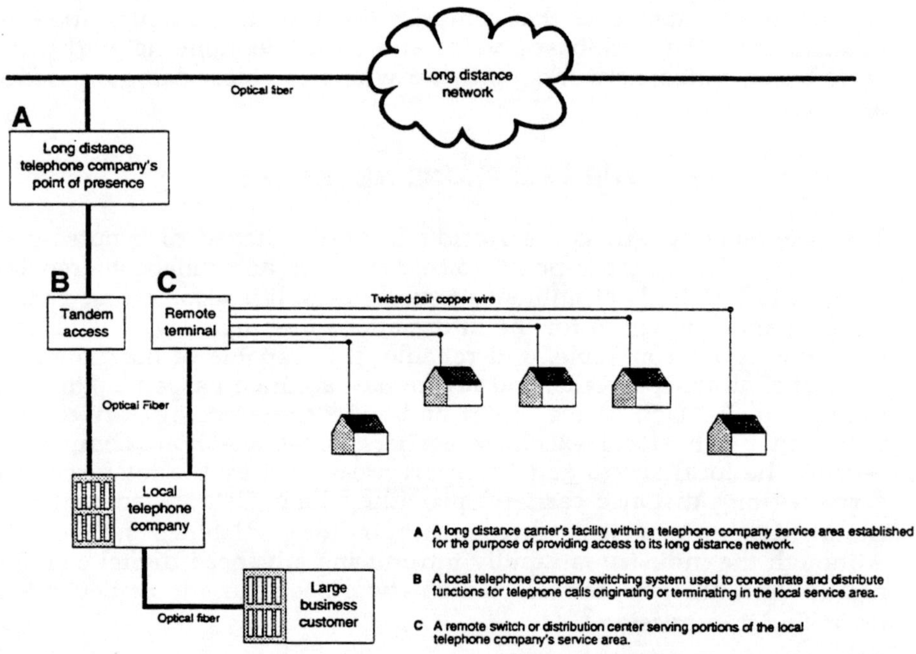

Source: Adapted from the "Hybridizing the Local Loop," Craig J. Burnet, IEEE Spectrum, June 1994.

Figure II.1: A typical local telephone network.

The telephone network's capabilities are unevenly distributed. Most of the high-capacity fiber optic lines capable carrying interactive video and other bandwidth-intensive applications are either part of the long distance or the local telephone area interoffice networks, or are used by the telephone companies to provide private voice, data and videoconferencing services to business, government, and institutions. The bandwidth available to residential subscribers is effectively constrained by the limited transmission capacity of the copper wire linking the local telephone company's central office with the subscriber's instrument, and the lack of subscriber's equipment capable of providing broadband services. Similarly, although the local telephone companies generally use digital switches to route telephone calls, in most cases the calls are converted back to analog format for transmission to individual subscribers. The basic architecture of a typical telephone network is shown in Figure II.1.

CABLE TELEVISION NETWORK

The nation's cable television network links thousands of cable systems with millions of subscribers via broadband coaxial cable.[3] This web of coaxial cables is, in many respects, a counterpart of the local loop linking telephone subscribers with the local telephone companies. However, there are considerable differences between the transmission technologies and network architectures deployed in the telephone and the cable systems.

The telephone system is based on a switched, distributed network architecture, and uses standard switching, and transmission protocols capable of supporting global, narrowband, two-way, point-to-point communications. The cable systems, on the other hand, are based on a tree-and-branch network architecture and proprietary transmission protocols designed to support one-way broadband analog transmission with little or no provision for "upstream" communications. The basic architecture of a typical cable system is shown in Figure II.2.

[3] During the last decade, the cable television industry experienced considerable growth, from 4,225 systems serving 17.7 million subscribers in 1980, to 11,075 cable systems serving over 57 million subscribers. Today, cable service - or ready access to the service provider's coaxial cable - is available to over 96 percent of the nation's home.

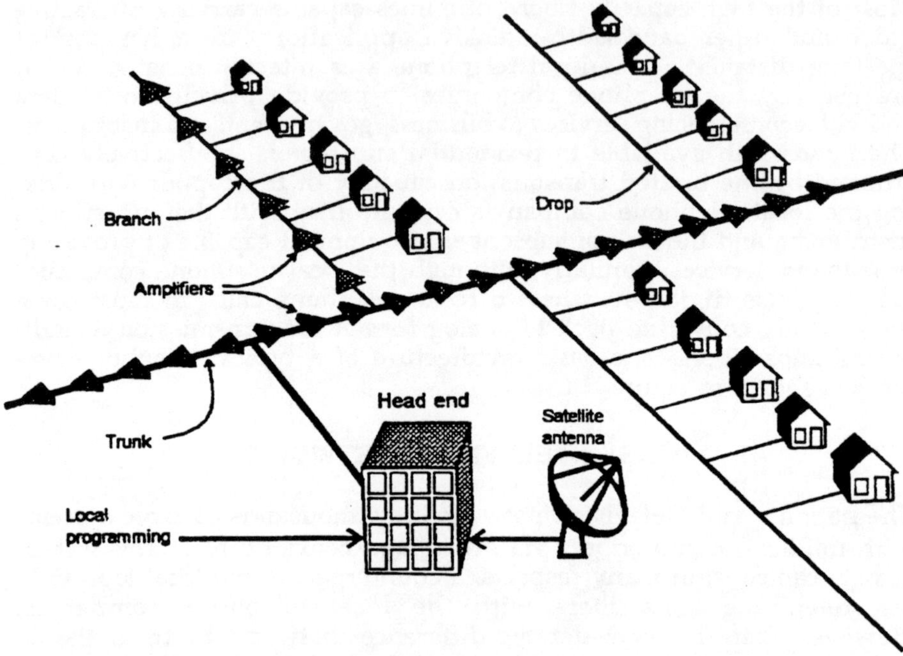

Figure II.2: A typical cable system architecture.

WIRELESS NETWORKS

Wireless networks are an important element of the communications infrastructure. These systems - including cellular and space-based systems and networks - are providing users with an unprecedented degree of mobility and flexibility. The cellular and satellite networks have advantages over terrestrial networks because they are potentially accessible from any point on the globe without the cost of installing wire or a cable. The current analog cellular services were developed in the early 1970s to alleviate growing radio frequency spectrum congestion and to overcome the limited capacity of the early mobile radio systems. In the cellular systems, this is accomplished by dividing a large geographic service area into discrete regions - or cells - each of which is served by a low-power base station transmitting to and receiving from mobile telephones within its area. The use of low-powered transmitters operating on short wavelengths allow the cellular systems to efficiently exploit the available radio spectrum by "reusing" the assigned radio frequencies throughout the service area.[4] However, the analog cellular systems have not fulfilled their early promise. In many large metropolitan markets, the systems are saturated and will be slowly supplemented, and eventually replaced, with digital systems.[5] The architecture of a typical cellular system is shown in Figure II.3.

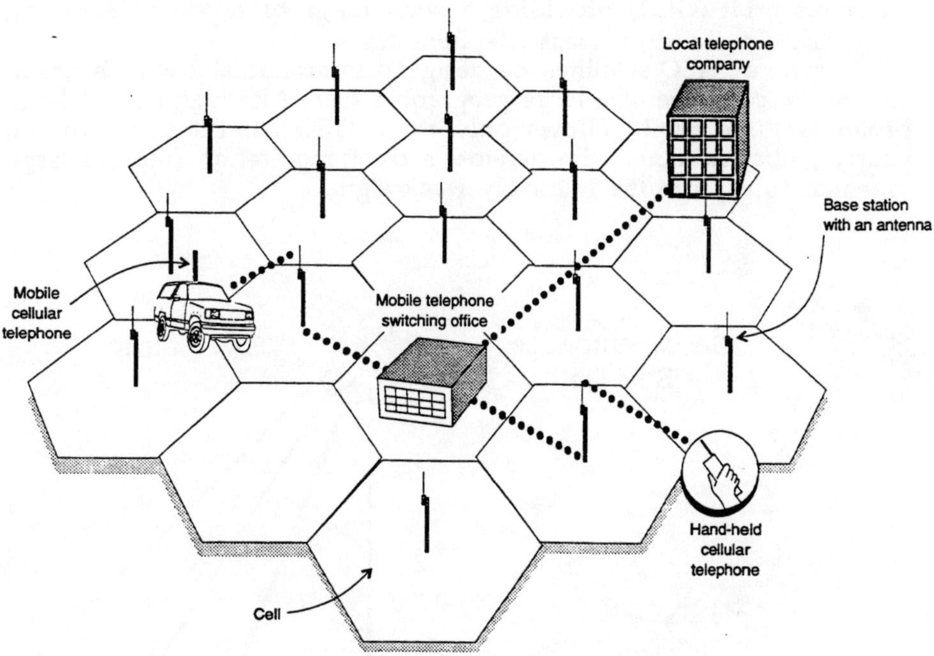

Figure II.3: A typical cellular system architecture.

---

[4] In the U.S. and in several other countries, the analog cellular systems are based on the Advanced Mobile Phone Services standard. This standard provides 416 voice channels and employs a seven-cell frequency reuse pattern.

[5] The FCC requires that any new digital cellular system be fully compatible with the current analog system. The new hand-held mobile units will be capable of either analog or digital operation.

Satellite networks have advantages over terrestrial networks because they are accessible from any spot on the globe; can provide broadband digital services, including voice, data, and video, to many points without the cost of acquiring right-of-way and cable installation; and can add receiving and transmitting sites without significant additional costs. Commercially available since 1965, communications satellites are a critical part of the global communications infrastructure. Today, there are about 150 communications satellites in geosynchronous orbit (GEO) providing a wide range of services, including broadcast video and overseas telephone links.[6]

In general, GEO satellites are designed to broadcast a wide beam to ensure the coverage of a large geographic area. Although such a large broadcast "footprint" allows only three GEO satellites to provide nearly global coverage, the network's receiving stations require large antennas to capture the relatively weak signal.

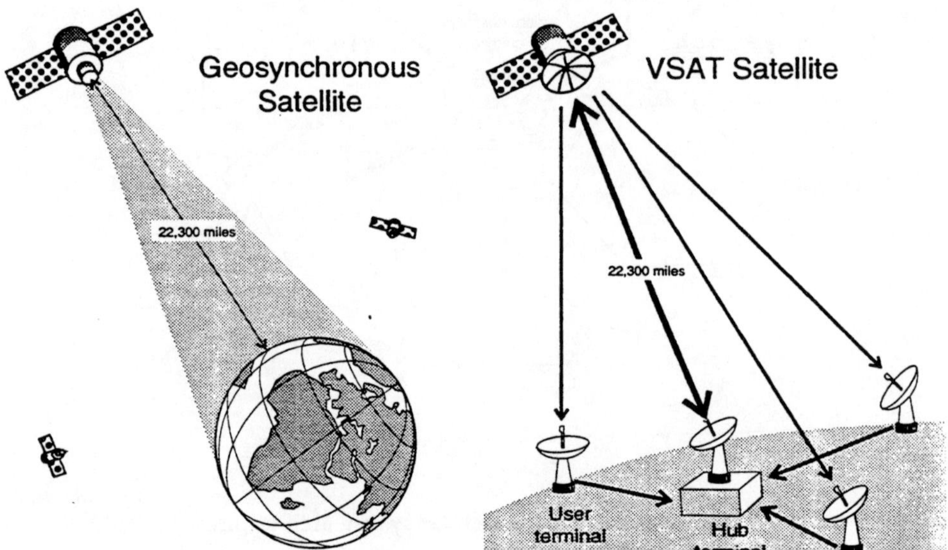

Figure II.4: Broadcast and VSAT Satellites.

---

[6] GEO satellites are placed in a high circular orbit 22,300 miles above the equator. Because GEO satellites rotate with the Earth, they appear to be stationary.

In the 1980s, industry introduced a new class of satellites using a narrow beam to focus the transmitted energy on a small geographic areas. Known as very small aperture terminal (VSAT) satellites, the new breed of satellites use small ground antennas to provide low data rate point-to-point network services. VSAT networks are being increasingly used by large corporations to link hundreds of motel/hotel or retail sites. Figure II.4 shows a typical GEO broadcast and VSAT satellite system based on a hub and spoke relay configuration. Because this configuration does not allow direct terminal-satellite-terminal relays, all communications must be routed through the hub terminal.

Appendix III

Description of Advanced Technologies

The communications industry is beginning to introduce several new and innovative technologies that will allow the delivery of many of the advanced services and capabilities of the information superhighway. These technologies include

- narrowband ISDN,
- advanced signaling and intelligent networks,
- B-ISDN,
- personal communications networks, and
- broadband in the local loop.

The Narrowband ISDN

One of the emerging technologies that will be key to the future superhighway is the narrowband ISDN. Deployment of this technology is the first step in the conversion from the existing networks to a fully digital network. ISDN is an end-to-end digital network that is evolving from the existing telephone network. It is already providing some users with direct access to digital transmissions - at speeds ranging from 144,000 bits per second (144 Kpbs) to 1.544 Mbps - capable of handling many different forms and types of information, including conventional analog voice, digital voice, and packet data.

Because of poorly defined standards, the early implementations of ISDN were plagued with interoperability problems. In an effort to effectively manage the integration of the ISDN technology with the public switched networks, the industry has adopted a set of standards known as the National ISDN. National ISDN will include advance signaling capabilities, as well as a wide range of digital services.

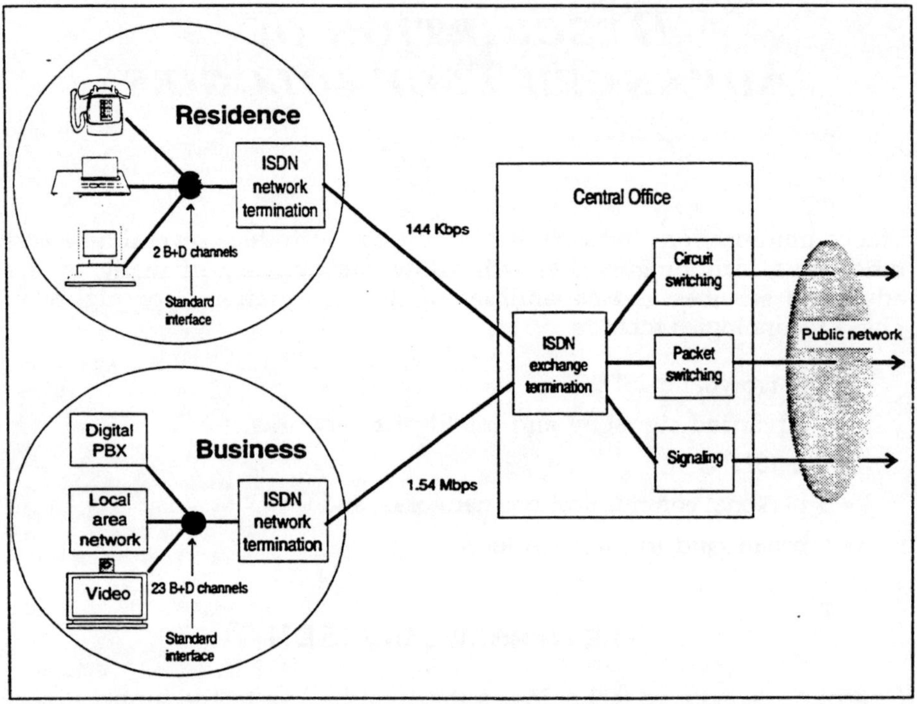

Figure III.1: ISDN architecture.

Telecommuting or work-at-home is one are where the benefits of ISDN service can be readily identified. Currently, an employee working at home may have to install additional telephone lines to handle computer and fax communications. Using ISDN, the telecommuter can communicate - over a single line - with the employer's local area network, while simultaneously carrying on a telephone conversation with a colleague and receiving a fax from the employer's office. Similarly, as shown in Figure III.1, a large business or institutional ISDN customer can use ISDN to consolidate voice, data, and videoconferencing services.

Advanced Signaling and Intelligent Networks

In order to offer new services and advanced capabilities, such as 800 number and ISDN services, the telephone industry is deploying common channel signaling networks. These networks are based on the Signaling System 7 (SS7) protocol. An SS7 network is a packet-switched communications network that transports call control and signaling messages on a dedicated high-speed data network separate from the voice or data

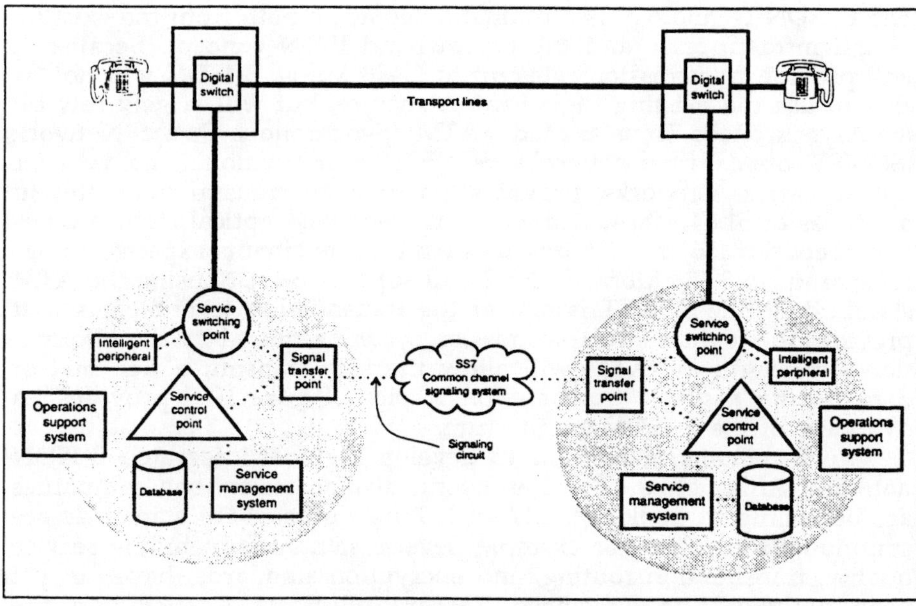

Source: Adapted from A Guide to New Technologies and Services, Bellcore, 1993; figure 1-1, pp. 1-5.

Figure III.2: AIN architecture

communications networks. The SS7 provides capabilities critical to the development of advanced intelligent networks (AIN). A programmable AIN network provides the capability for network switches to interrogate remote processors, databases, and mobile communications devices. The network intelligence resides in one-line, real-time databases, rather than in every switch, and is accessed through the SS7 signaling system. Such intelligent networks allow greater customer control, provide the tools for the creation of virtual private networks, increase competition by allowing competing carriers to use the AIN capabilities to offer custom services, and provide the mechanisms for alternative call destination routing required by the emerging personal communications services (PCS).[1] Figure III.2 shows a simplified view of an AIN architecture.

B-ISDN Technologies

The B-ISDN technology is a dramatic departure both from the existing digital infrastructure and the narrowband ISDN concept. Because it will provide transmission rates up to 2,488 Mbps, B-ISDN will not be able to use the existing digital infrastructure, but will largely rely on the Asynchronous Transfer Mode (ATM)/Synchronous Optical Network (SONET) optical fiber networks. SONET, an international standard for optical carrier networks, provides a variety of transmission rates in multiples of 51.84 Mbps, with currently deployed optical circuits operating between 156 to 622 Mbps, and with future circuits expected to operate at up to 2,488 Mbps. SONET will support B-ISDN using the ATM standard. While SONET is one of the transmission technologies that provides the highs-speed transmission system required by the information superhighway, ATM will allow users to transmit a rich mix of data during a single transmission session. Figure III.3 provides an overview of the B-ISDN architecture.

Much remains to be done to develop a global integrated B-ISDN network. Although the local and long distance telephone companies are beginning to deploy ATM/SONET networks, ATM standards are continuing to evolve. For example, several standards including service quality, transmission routing, and encryption standards, have not yet been defined. The Advanced Research Projects Agency and the National Science Foundation, in coordination with industry, are actively pursuing investigations focused on the development of ATM

[1] PCS is a new type of service designed to support hand-held personal voice and data communications terminals. Mobile PCS users are expected to be able to receive services such as high-quality voice, data, facsimile, and video at any terminal anywhere the user has directed his or her calls.

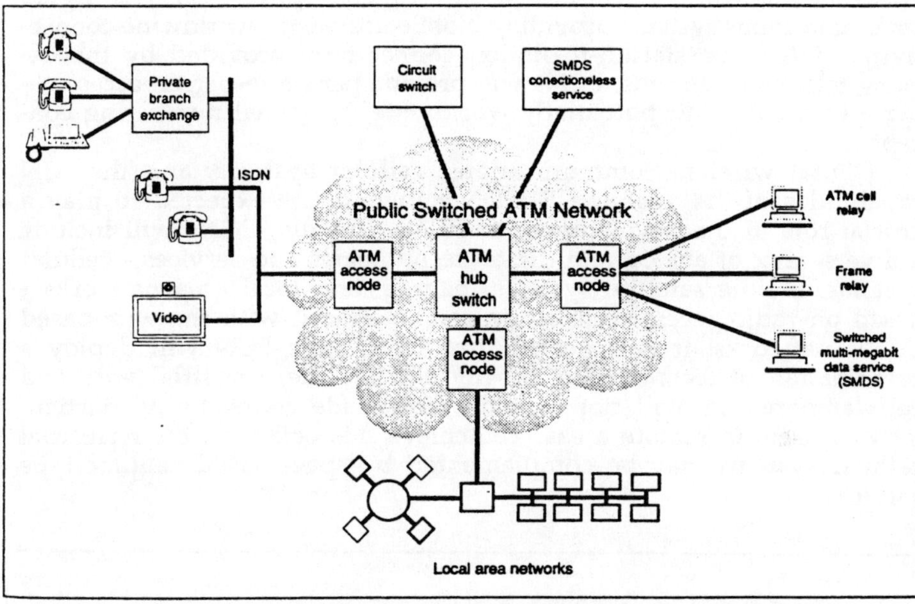

Source: Adapted from A Guide to New Technologies and Services, Bellcore, 1993; figure 2-6, pp. 2-11.

Figure III.3: B-ISDN architecture.

standards and network management tools. These two agencies established five gigabit network research testbeds focused on ATM network technology, alternative network architectures, and applications. In addition, the Advanced Research Projects Agency is evaluating the best commercial prototypes of ATM/SONET technology and related applications, including ATM satellite connections and the encryption of gigabit data streams.

Personal Communications Networks

Some observers believe that we are moving toward a ubiquitous, tetherless global metanetwork composed of cellular and satellite communications systems supplemented by wire-based ground networks. Personal communications networks (PCN) and the related personal communications services (PCS) are expected to be an important part of this tetherless metanetwork. PCNs are based on a concept of tetherless digital communications systems providing mobile users with worldwide connectivity. Unlike the station-to-station connectivity provided by the existing telephone systems, PCNs will provide person-to-person access using a national - and potentially worldwide - personal numbering concept.

Digital wireless communications, cellular systems, and the AIN capabilities of the evolving B-ISDN networks are expected to play a crucial role in the development of PCNs. Initially, PCNs will include a diverse mix of analog and digital technologies and services - cellular systems, mobile satellite systems, paging, and local area networks - based on radio access technology and interfaced with the wire-based public networks. It is expected that a full-scale PCN will deploy a combination of technologies, mostly because the terrestrial wire and cellular networks will not provide worldwide connectivity, particularly to users in remote areas. To achieve this objective, the terrestrial cellular systems may be complemented by space-based cellular type services.

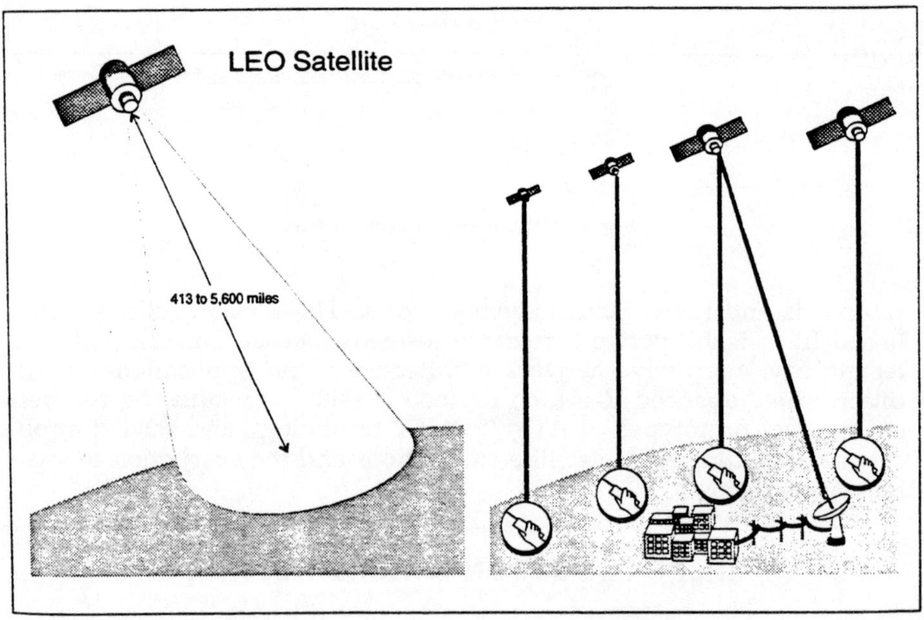

Figure III.4: Low earth orbit satellite system

There are two basic approaches to space-based PCNs. One uses satellites in high geosynchronous earth orbit (GEO), while the other relies on a constellation of low-earth orbit (LEO) satellites. The GEO systems, being in higher orbit, require more power at both the transmitter and the receiver than the LEOs, but provide more earth coverage with fewer spacecraft. On the other hand, LEO systems, while cheaper on a unit-basis, require far more satellites to provide earth coverage. In general, most of the recently proposed space-based PCNs are focused on LEO systems, including Motorola's Iridium system (77 satellites), TRW's Odyssey system (12 satellites), Leosat's system (18 satellites), and the recently announced network of 840 satellites proposed by the Teledesic Corp. Figure III.4 show a typical LEO satellite network.

BROADBAND IN THE LOCAL LOOP

While industry is upgrading the transport layer and laying thousands of miles of optical fiber, the on-ramps that will link the high-speed portions of the national information infrastructure with homes, business, and institutions continue to form a bottleneck to high-speed information flow. In the near term, the primary challenge will be to provide broadband digital services over the existing plant - the hundreds of thousands of miles of copper wire and coaxial cable - although ultimately it may be preferable to provide fiber optics to each residence. The replacement cost for this "last mile" of the superhighway - linking the broadband backbone with residences, business and institutions - continues to be high, not only because there is so much copper wire and coaxial cable to be replaced, but also because of the need for special equipment to process the optical signal on the customer's premises.

The telephone and cable companies are adopting a mix of technologies and strategies to cope with the bottleneck in the local loop - the portion of the telephone communication circuit connecting individual subscribers with the telephone company's central office. For the telephone companies, the most promising approaches are the asymmetrical digital subscriber line and the fiber-to-the-curb architectures. The asymmetrical digital subscriber line allows telephone companies to use a single copper wire to simultaneously transmit video and telephone signals by increasing the transmission speed from 64 Kpbs to 1.5 Mbps while providing an upstream channel between 16 to 384 Kbps. The fiber-to-the-curb architecture provides high-capacity switched digital network services to optical network units serving multiple residences. Optical network units house the necessary equipment to convert the optical signals to electrical impulses and distribute them to individual homes over a copper wire or coaxial cable.

Most of the newer or rebuilt cable systems also use a hybrid fiber optics/coaxial cable architecture, commonly known as fiber trunk feeder. This hybrid fiber optics/coaxial cable architecture is capable of supporting all digital, fully switched ATM/SONET services. Figure III.5 highlights two fiber-to-the-curb architectures that may be used by the telephone and cable industries to deliver broadband services to subscribers.

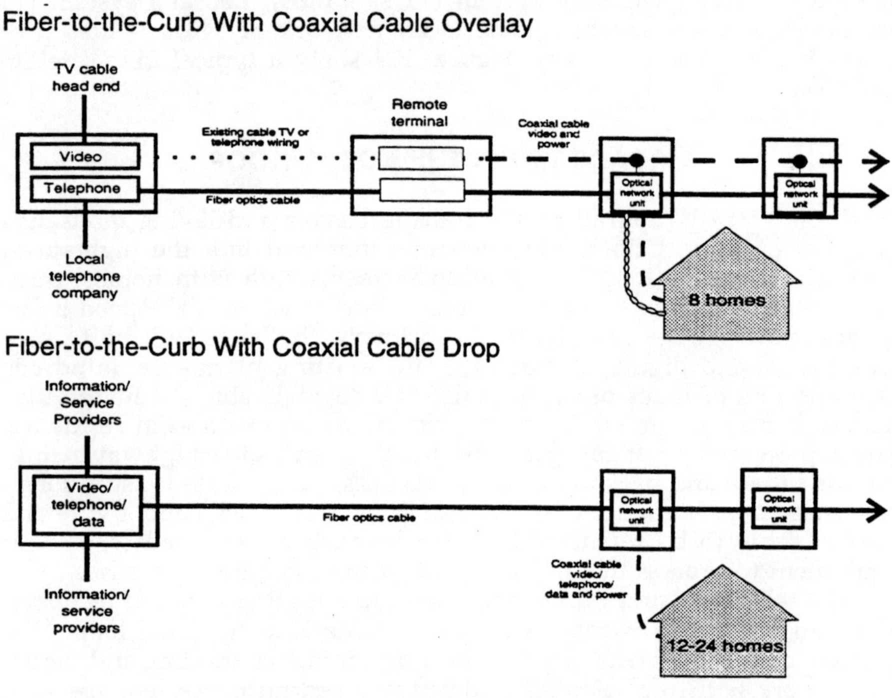

Figure III.5: Broadband in the local loop.

Appendix IV

Ensuring the Portability of Telephone Numbers Poses a Challenge

The ability of the public networks to efficiently route and deliver electronic communications is heavily dependent on the efficient allocation and use of limited resource - the pool of available ten-digit telephone numbers. In recent years, the proliferation of telecommunications services and providers has placed increasing demands on this resource. More importantly, new requirements, such as demands for (1) personal mobility, whereby communications services are provided to individuals, rather than to fixed geographic locations (for example geographic mobility), and (2) number portability, whereby customers are able to change service features and providers quickly *without* needing to change their telephone number, will significantly alter the way we manage the numbering resources.

The first demand - the provision of services to individuals rather than fixed geographic locations - will be largely satisfied by emerging PCSs, PCSs will exploit the capabilities of AIN and nongeographic telephone numbers to provide wireless or land-line based services to "roaming" individuals. The second demand - the assignment of a permanent "personal" telephone number to individuals - will require the development of national or regional databases containing the personal numbers and customer service profiles. Although there are no insurmountable technical barriers to number portability, industry's experience with the development of full portability for the 800 number services indicates that it will be a lengthy and arduous process.[1]

[1] It took almost 7 years for industry to implement full portability for 800 service.

THE NORTH AMERICAN NUMBERING PLAN GUIDES THE MANAGEMENT OF NUMBERING RESOURCES

The basic telephone numbering scheme, known as the North American Numbering Plan (NANP), was developed the Bell System. In 1984, following the AT&T divestiture, the numbering plan functions performed by AT&T were transferred to Bell Communications Research (Bellcore). Since that time, Bellcore has served as the NANP administrator. Under NANP, each telephone within the World Zone 1[2] can be reached by dialing a unique ten-digit number generally composed of three parts - a three-digit geographic area code, a three-digit secondary code, and a four-digit "station" or "line" code.

However, under the current format, there are only 160 possible area codes. These represent the number of combinations available when the first digit cannot be zero or one, and the second digit is always zero or one. Sixteen of the codes have a unique format: eight have a double "0" ("N00" codes) and eight have a double "1" ("N11" codes). The N00 codes are called Service Access Codes (SAC).[3] The most widely recognized SACs are the 800 and 900 codes. The N11 codes are known as "service codes" and are set aside for special functions, the most widely used being the 911 emergency code. All of the remaining 144 codes are assigned and it has been long expected that the present stock of codes would be exhausted sometime in the 1990s.

A numbering relief plan, scheduled to be implemented in January 1995, will expand the number of potential codes from 160 to 800. This expansion will be accomplished by allowing the second digit of the area code to include the digits "2" through "9" in addition to "1" and "0". For example, area code 334 is scheduled to be placed in service in northern Alabama on January 15, 1995. The addition of 640 new codes will not only significantly increase the numbering resource, but may also provide additional codes for nongeographic assignment such as the "personal" numbers needed for PCS users. Because the new codes will not be available until 1995, carriers anxious to offer PCS asked Bellcore for the assignment of one of the four nongeographic codes (500 SAC) for PCS. The carriers plan to offer PCS that includes personal mobility, terminal mobility, and service profile services, but not, at least ini-

---

[2] The World Zone 1 includes the United States, Canada, Bermuda and most of the Caribbean. It provides a uniform dialing scheme applicable in 18 countries, and serves more than a thousand local exchange carriers, several hundred long distance carriers, and over one hundred million customers. International calls to countries not included in the NANP require the dialing of country codes; thus telephone numbers can differ in length from country to country.

[3] Three SACs (700, 800 and 900) are currently in use through World Zone 1; one (600) is assigned to the Canadian government, while the 500 SAC has been assigned for roaming PCS.

tially, number portability. In essence, PCS users would have to be issued a new telephone number every time they changed a PCS provider.

PORTABILITY ISSUES REMAIN UNRESOLVED

In June 1993, Bellcore informed the FCC that it had decided, absent instructions to the contrary, to proceed with the assignment of 500 SAC for PCS service to carriers that had expressed an urgent need for these assignments. In response to Bellcore's notification, the FCC requested public comments on the proposed assignment of the 500 SAC for PCS, and directed Bellcore to delay the assignments until it had a chance to consider the comments. At the same time, FCC asked Bellcore to submit, within 30 days, a detailed proposal for achieving 500 number portability. In response, Bellcore noted that there were many ways to achieve number portability, but did not offer a concrete proposal. An industry workgroup is addressing the issue of PCS number portability. Bellcore began assigning numbering resources within the 500 SAC for roaming services after the FCC considered the comments on the issue and gave its approval in May 1994. Bellcore also notified the FCC that because of the many changes in the telecommunications environment which have resulted in increased controversy regarding numbering, Bellcore and its owners believed that it was time it relinquish Bellcore's voluntary administration of the NANP.

The FCC has yet to take final action in finding a replacement for Bellcore or to act on the 500 SAC portability issues. According to the United States Telephone Association, it appears unlikely that the initial PCS services will provide number portability. Full national number portability may not be available for years, given that the design and deployment of a database architecture for the 500 SAC will take considerable time.

Glossary

Address	A sequence of bits or characters that identifies the destination and the source of a transmission.
Advanced Intelligent Network	An evolving architecture that allows rapid creation and modification of telecommunications services.
Agile Manufacturing	An approach to industrial production that allows a manufacturer to rapidly respond to market demand by reducing the time it takes to design and manufacture a product. Also known as rapid response or demand activated manufacturing.
Amplitude	A relative magnitude of a signal.
Analog	A term applied to any device, usually electronic, that represents values by a continuously variable physical property, such as voltage in an electronic circuit. An analog device can represent an infinite number of values within the range the device can handle. In contrast, digital representation maps values onto discrete numbers, limiting the possible range of values to the resolution of the digital device.
Analog Signal	A continuous electrical signal whose amplitude varies in direct correlation with the original input.

Architecture A general term referring to the structure of all or part of a computer system. The term also covers the design of system software, such as the operating system, as well as refers to the combination of hardware and basic software that links the machines on a computer network. Computer architecture refers to an entire structure and to the details needed to make it functional. Thus, computer architecture covers computer systems, chips, circuits, and system programs, but typically does not cover applications, which are required to perform a task but not to make the system run.

Asynchronous Operation Generally, an operation that proceeds independently of any timing mechanism, such as a clock. In communications, for example, two modems communicating asynchronously rely upon each one sending the other start and stop signals in order to pace the exchange of information.

Asynchronous Transfer Mode A fast-packet technology that was developed for use in area networks using fixed length cells. Current ATM standards allow it to scale from speeds of 15 Mbps to 622 Mbps over fiber networks. ATM appears to be the best alternative for multimedia applications where data are mixed with voice, images, or full-motion video.

Bandwidth In communications, the difference between the highest and lowest frequencies in a given range. For example, a telephone accommodates a bandwidth of 3000 hertz (Hz), the difference between the lowest (300 Hz) and highest (3300 Hz) frequencies it can carry. In computer networks, greater bandwidth indicates faster data-transfer capabilities.

Basic Rate Interface Transmission rate for the integrated service digital network. Basic rate interface consists of two 64 Kbps channels and one 16 Kbps channel packet-switched data channel used for signaling and packet data transmission functions.

Bit Short for "Binary Digit"; either 1 or 0 in the binary number system. In processing and storage, a bit is the smallest unit of information handled by a computer and is represented physically by an element such as a single pulse sent through a circuit or a small spot on a magnetic disk capable of storing either a 1 or a 0. Considered singly, bits convey little information a human would consider meaningful. In groups of eight, however, bits become the familiar bytes used to represent all types of information, including the letters of the alphabet and the digits.

Broadband Network A type of local area network on which transmissions travel as radio-frequency signals over separate inbound and outbound channels. Stations on a broadband network are connected by coaxial or fiber-optic cable. The cable itself can be made to carry data, voice, and video simultaneously over multiple transmission channels. This complex transmission is accomplished by the technique called frequency-division multiplexing, in which individual channels are separated by frequency and buffered from one another by guard bands of frequencies that are not used for transmission.

Capstone Chip A data security chip. The Capstone chip, also known as MYK-80, incorporates NSA's Skipjack, key exchange algorithms, and the NIST digital signature and secure hash algorithms.

Cell	In cellular systems, the smallest geographic area defined for mobile communications systems.
Cellular Systems	Mobile telephony systems employing hexagonal geographic areas, or cells, with group frequencies allocated to each cell. Typically, seven cells make a block, and no adjacent cell uses the same set of frequencies.
Ciphertext	The encrypted form of a plaintext message or data.
Circuit Switching	A method of opening communications lines, as through the telephone system, creating a physical link between the initiating and receiving parties. In circuit switching, the connection is made at a switching center, which physically connects the two parties and maintains an open line between them for as long as needed. Circuit switching is typically used in modem communications on the dial-up telephone network, and it is also used on a smaller scale in privately maintained communications networks.
Clipper Chip	A microcircuit that contains a classified secret-key encryption algorithm known as Skipjack. The Clipper chip family, manufactured by Mykotronx, Inc., includes three prototypes chips - the MYK-78E, MYK-78T, and MYK-77.MYK-78E and MYK-78T are designed for wirebased digital telephony. MYK-77 is designed for use in digital radios operating at low data rates. Also see Capstone Chip.

Coaxial Cable Often referred to as coax or coax cable. A cable that consists of two conductors, a center wire inside a cylindrical shield that is grounded. The shield is typically made of braided wire and is insulated from the center wire. The shield minimizes electrical and radio-frequency interference; signals in a coaxial cable do not affect nearby components, and potential interference from these components does not affect the signal carried on the cable.

Code Division Multiple Access A cellular digital standard that deploys frequency hopping - rapid change of frequency - with the carrier frequency continually shifted through a wideband channel.

Common Channel Signaling A method of carrying signaling and supervisory information between telephone central offices in a separate, dedicated channel.

Communications Protocol A set of rules or standards designed to enable computers to connect with one another and to exchange information with as little error as possible. The word "protocol" is used, sometimes confusingly, in reference to a multitude of standards affecting different aspects of communication. Some standards affect hardware connections, while other standards govern data transmission. Still other protocols govern file transfer, and others define the methods by which messages are passed around the stations on a local area network. Taken as a whole, these various and sometimes conflicting protocols represent attempts to facilitate communication among computers of different makes and models.

Computer Network A group of computers and associated devices that are connected by communications facilities. A network can involve permanent connections, such as cables, or temporary connections made through telephone or other communication links. A network can be as small as a local area network consisting of a few computers, printers, and other devices, or it can consist of many small and large computers distributed over a vast geographic area. Small or large, a computer network exists to provide computer users with the means of communicating and transferring information electronically. Some types of communication are simple user-to-user messages; others, of the type known as distributed processes, can involve several computers and the sharing of workloads or cooperative efforts in performing a task.

Cryptanalysis The process of converting encrypted messages into plaintext without knowledge of the key employed in the encryption algorithm.

Cryptographic Algorithm A mathematical procedure used for such purposes as encrypting and decrypting messages and signing documents digitally.

Cryptographic System The hardware, software, documents, and associated techniques and processes that together provide a means of encryption.

Cryptography The transformation of ordinary test - or plaintext - and other data into coded form by encryption and the transformation of the coded text or data back to plaintext or data by decryption.

Data Encryption Standard A NIST Federal Information Processing Standard and a commonly used secret-key cryptographic algorithm for encrypting and decrypting data.

Digital Related to digits or the way they are represented. In computing, *digital* is virtually synonymous with *binary* because the computers familiar to most people process information coded as combinations of binary digits, or bits - zeros and ones. One bit can represent at most two values - 0 or 1. Two bits can represent up to 4 different values - 00, 01, 11 and 10. Eight bits can represent 256 values - 00000000, 00000001, 00000011, and so on.

Digital Signature A cryptographic method, provided by public-key cryptography, used by a message's recipient or any third party to verify the identity of the message's sender and the integrity of the message. A sender creates a digital signature or a message by transforming the message with his or her private key. A recipient, using the sender's public key, verifies the digital signature by applying a corresponding transformation to the message and the signature.

Digital Signature Standard A NIST Federal Information Processing Standard that supports digital signature.

Electronic Signature See digital signature.

Encryption The transformation of data into a form readable only by using the appropriate key, held only by authorized parties. The key rearranges the data into its original form by reversing the encryption.

Escrow Encryption Standard
A Federal Information Processing Standard specifying technology that provides a mechanism for the secure escrow of encryption keys, which can be used to intercept message only by government officials acting under proper legal authorization. The standard relies on a key escrow chip, known as Clipper, programmed with the classified Skipjack algorithm. Also see Clipper Chip, Capstone Chip, Skipjack, key escrow system, private key, public key cryptography.

Fiber-Optics
A method of transmitting light beams along optical fibers. A light beam, such as that produced in a laser, can be modulated to carry information. A single fiber-optic channel can carry significantly more information than most other means of information transmission. Optical fibers are thin strands of glass or other transparent material.

Frame Relay
A type of fast packet technology using variable length packets called frames. By contrast, a cell relay system, such as ATM, transports user data in fixed-sized cells.

Geosynchronous Orbit
The orbit of a satellite in which the speed and path are precisely timed to position it 22,300 miles over a fixed location on Earth.

Giga
A prefix for one billion (10^9) times a specific unit.

Gigabyte
The precise meaning often varies with the context; strictly, a gigabyte is 1 billion bytes. In reference to computers, however, bytes are often expressed in multiples of powers of two. Therefore, a gigabyte can also be either 1,000 megabytes or 1,024 megabytes, where a megabyte is considered to be 1,048,576 bytes.

Hacker	A person who accesses or attempts to access a computer without authorization. For the purpose of this report, the term hacker refers to an external threat of unauthorized access to communications networks and related systems.
Hash Function	A technique for computing a hash total. Hash total is an error-checking value derived from the addition of a set of numbers taken from text or data. In cryptography, the recipient may use the hash function to verify a message's integrity by recalculating and verifying the hash total. If the two do not match, the original information has been changed in some way.
Hertz	A unit of frequency equal to one cycle per second.
Information Superhighway	A popular term for the emerging global broadband digital metanetwork. Also known as the national information infrastructure, infobahn, or global grid.
Interactive	Operating in a back-and-forth, often conversational manner, as when a user enters a question or command and the system immediately responds. Microcomputers are interactive machines; this interactivity is one of the features that make them approachable and easy to use.
International Data Encryption Algorithm	A block-encryption algorithm that operates on 64 bits of plaintext at a time. Developed by James Massay and Xuejia Lai at ETH, a technical institute in Zurich, the International Data Encryption Algorithm (IDEA) is perceived as a potential replacement for Data Encryption Standard. Also see Pretty Good Privacy.

Internet	Abbreviation for "internetwork." In communications, a set of computer networks - possibly dissimilar - joined together by means of gateways that handle data transfer and the conversion of messages from the sending network to the protocols used by the receiving network (with packets if necessary). When capitalized, the term "Internet" refers to the collection of networks and gateways that use the Transmission Control Protocol/Internet Protocol suite of protocols.
Interoperability	The ability of two or more systems or components to exchange information and to use the information that has been exchanged.
ISDN	Abbreviation for "Integrated Services Digital Network" - a worldwide digital communications network evolving from existing telephone services. The goal of ISDN is to replace the current analog telephone system with totally digital switching and transmission facilities capable of carrying data ranging from voice to computer transmissions, music, and video. ISDN is built in two main types of communications channels; a B channel, which carries data at a rate of 64 Kbps (kilobits per second) and a D channel, which carries control information at either 16 or 64 Kbps. Computers and other devices are connected to ISDN lines through simple, standardized interfaces. When fully implemented (possibly around the turn of the century), ISDN is expected to provide users with fast, more extensive communications services.
Japanese Digital Cellular	A Japanese standard for digital cellular services.

Key	A long stream of seemingly random bits used with cryptographic algorithms. The keys must be known or guessed to forge a digital signature or decrypt an encrypted message.
Key Escrow System	A mechanism for the secure escrow, and controlled release, of secret or private encryption keys to law enforcement officials. Also see Escrow Encryption Standard.
Kilo	A prefix for one thousand (10^3) times a specific unit.
Last Mile	A popular term for the last segment of the connection between a communication provider and the customer. Also see local loop and on-ramps.
Local Area Network	A group of computers and other devices dispersed over a relatively limited area and connected by a communications link that enables a device to interact with any other on the network. Local area networks (LANs) commonly include microcomputers and shared (often expensive) resources such as laser printers and large hard disks. Most modern LANs can support a wide variety of computers and other devices. Each device must use the proper physical and data-link protocols for the particular LAN, and all devices that want to communicate with each other on the LAN must use the same upper-level communications protocol. Although single LANs are geographically limited (to a department or an office building for example), separate LANs can be connected to form larger networks. Similar LANs are linked by bridges that act as transfer points between networks, dissimilar LANs are linked by gateways, which both transfer data and convert it according to the protocols used by the receiving network.

Local Loop	A communication circuit connecting the telephone company central office with a subscriber's instrument. Also see last mile and on-ramps.
Mega	Abbreviated M. A prefix meaning 1 million (10^6). In computing, which is based on the binary (base-2) numbering system, *mega* has a literal value of 1,048,576 which is the power of 2 closest to one million.
Megabit	Abbreviated Mb or Mbit. Usually, 1,048,576 bits; sometimes interpreted as 1 million bits.
Megabyte	Abbreviated MB. Either 1 million bytes or 1,048,576 bytes.
Metanetwork	A "super" network connecting many other networks. A network of networks.
Mobile Communications	A European standard for digital cellular services.
Multicast	A variant of broadcast, where information can be sent to selected recipients instead of all subscribers of a particular communications system.
Multimedia	A popular term for the integration of information in a single format, for example an electronic document that may contain text, embedded voice, video, or images.
Narrowband Network	A flexible, all purpose, two-way medium that supports transmission rates under 1.5 Mbp. Also see broadband network.
National Information Infrastructure	The administration's term for the information superhighway.

Network Architecture The underlying structure of a computer network, including hardware, functional layers, interfaces, and protocols (rules) used to establish communications and ensure the reliable transfer of information. Because a computer network is a mixture of hardware and software, network architectures are designed to provide both philosophical and physical standards for enabling computers and other devices to handle the complexities of establishing communications links and transferring information without conflict. Various network architectures exist, among them the internationally accepted seven-layer open systems interconnection model and International Business Machine (IBM) Systems Network Architecture. Both the open systems interconnection model and the Systems Network Architecture organize network functions in layers, each layer dedicated to a particular aspect of communication or transmission and each requiring protocols that define how functions are carried out.

Nodes The devices on a LAN are known as nodes, and the nodes are connected by cables through which messages are transmitted. Types of cables include twisted-pair wiring, coaxial cable, or fiber-optic (light-transmitting) cable. Nodes on a LAN can be wired together in any of three basic layouts, known as bus, ring, and star. As implied by their names, a bus network is more or less linear, a ring network forms a loop, and a star network radiates from a central hub.

North American Dual-Mode Cellular System A North American standard for digital cellular services.

On Ramp A popular term for a digital broadband connection linking a subscriber with the information superhighway. Also see local loop and last mile.

Operating System The software responsible for controlling the allocation and usage of hardware resources such as memory, the central processing unit, disk space, and peripheral devices.

Optical Fiber A lightguide for electromagnetic waves traveling in the infrared and visible light spectrum. An optical fiber consists of two different types of glass, core and cladding, surrounded by a protective coating. The core is the light-guiding region of the fiber, while the cladding ensures that the light pulses remain within the core. One mile of fiber, capable of transmission speeds of 2,500 Mbps (2.5 gigabits per second) weighs about 1/7 of a pound. A copper cable with the same information-carrying capacity would weigh 33 tons.

Packet In general usage, a unit of information transmitted as a whole from one device to another on a network. In packet-switching networks, a packet is defined more specifically as a transmission unit of fixed maximum size that consists of binary digits representing both data and a header containing an identification number, source and destination addresses, and, sometimes, error-control data

Packet Switching A message-delivery technique in which small units of information (packets) are relayed through stations in a computer network along the best route currently available between the source and the destination. A packet-switching network handles information in small units, breaking long messages into multiple packets before routing. Although each packet may travel along a different path, and the packets composing a message may arrive at different times or out of sequence, the receiving computer reassembles the original message. Packet-switching networks are considered to be fast and efficient. To manage the tasks of routing traffic and assembling/disassembling packets, such networks require some "intelligence" from the computers and software that control delivery.

Personal Communications Network Advanced cellular communications and the internetworking of both wire and wireless networks that are expected to offer new communications services via very small portable handsets. The network will rely on microcellular technology – many low-power, small-coverage cells and a common channel signaling technology, to provide a wide variety of features in addition to the basic two-way telephone service.

Plaintext Plain, unencrypted text or data

Point of Presence A long distance carrier's network access facility located within the service area of a local telephone company.

Pretty Good Privacy A cryptographic software application for the protection of computer files and electronic mail. It combines the convenience of the Rivest-Shamir-Adelman public key algorithm with the speed of the secret-key IDEA algorithm, digital signature, and key management. It was developed by Philip Zimmerman, and is available globally as freeware from Internet sites or as commercial software.

Primary Rate Interface A transmission rate interface for the integrated service digital network. It consists of 23 64 Kbps channels and one 64 Kbps channel used for signaling. Six of the 64 Kbps channels can be combined into a single 384 Kbps channel, or 24 64 Kbps channels can be combined to form a single 1.536 Mbps channel. These bundles can support applications requiring high data rates, such as video or host-to-host bulk data transfers.

Private Branch Exchange A private telephone exchange connected to the public telephone network.

Private Key The undisclosed key in a matched key pair – private key and public key – used in public key cryptographic systems.

Public Key The key in a matched key pair – private key and public key – that is made public, for example, posted in a public directory, for public key cryptography.

Public Key Cryptography Cryptography using two matched keys (or asymmetric cryptography) in which a single private key is not shared by a pair of users. Instead, each user has a key pair. Each key pair consists of a private key that is kept secret by the user and a public key that is posted in a public directory. I Public key cryptography is used to perform (1) digital signature, (2) secure transmission or exchange of secret keys, and/or (3) encryption and decryption.

Real-Time System A computer and/or a software system that reacts to events before the events become obsolete. For example, airline collision avoidance systems must process radar input, detect a possible collision, and warn air traffic controllers or pilots while they still have time to react.

Rivest-Shamir-Adelman A public key algorithm invented by Ronald L. Rivest, Adi Shamir, and Leonard M. Adelman. The algorithm can be used to generate digital signatures, encrypt messages, and provide key management for Data Encryption Standard and other secret key algorithms.

Secret Key The single key that two or more parties share and keep secret for secret key cryptography. Given secret key algorithms of equal strength, the approximate difficulty of decrypting encrypted messages by brute force search can be measured by the number of possible keys. For example, a key length of 56 bits is over 66,000 times stronger or more resistant to attack than a key length of 40 bits.

Secret Key Cryptography Cryptography based on a single key (or symmetric cryptography). It uses the same secret key for encryption and decryption.

Signaling The process of generating and exchanging information between components of telecommunications systems to establish, monitor, or release connections (call handling functions) and to control related network and system operations and functions.

Signaling System 7 An international common channel signaling system.

Skipjack A classified encryption algorithm. Skipjack provides high-speed encryption when implemented in a Clipper chip.

Standard	In computing, a set of detailed technical guidelines used as a means of establishing uniformity in an area of hardware or software development. Computer standards have traditionally developed in either of two ways. The first, a highly informal process, occurs when a product or philosophy is developed by a single company and, through success and imitation, becomes so widely used that deviation from the norm causes compatibility problems or limits marketability. This type of de facto standard setting is typified by such products as Hayes modems and IBM Personal Computers. The second type of standard setting is a far more formal process in which specifications are drafted by a cooperative group or committee after an intensive study of existing methods, approaches, and technological trends and developments. The proposed standards are later ratified by consensus through an accredited organization and are adopted over time as products based on the standards become increasingly prevalent in the market
Synchronous Operation	Generally, any operation that proceeds under control of a clock or timing mechanism.
Synchronous Optical Network (SONET)	An international standard for transmitting information over optical fiber at high speeds.
Synchronous Transmission	The serial transmission of a bit stream in which each bit occurs at a fixed time interval and the entire stream is preceded by a specific combination of bits that initiate the timing.

T-Carrier System	A hierarchy of digital transmission capabilities designed to operate at various rates, designated T1 (1.544 Mbps), T2 (6.312 Mbps), T3 (44.736 Mbps), and T4 (274.176 Mbps).
Telecommunications	A general term for the electronic transmission of information of any type, including data, television pictures, sound, facsimiles, and so on.
Telecommuting	Also called electronic commuting. The practice of working in one location (often, at home) and communicating with a main office in a different location through a personal computer equipped with a modem and communications software.
Time Division Multiple Access	A digital encoding scheme used in cellular service, this transmission method allows users to simultaneously transmit on the same frequency by allocating each user a discrete time slot.
Trojan Horse	A computer program that conceals harmful code. A Trojan horse usually masquerades as a useful program that a user would wish to execute.
Twisted-Pair Wire	A wire made of two separately insulated strands of wire twisted together.
Virus	A computer program that can infect, replicate, and spread among computer systems. Unlike the computer worm, a virus requires human involvement (usually unwitting) to propagate.
Wide Area Network	A communications network that connects geographically separated areas.
Wiretapping	The real-time collection of transmitted voice or data, and the sending of that data in real time to a listening device. ("Real time" is defined as the actual time that something, such as communication of information, takes place.)

Worm -	An independent computer program that reproduces by copying itself from one system to another while traveling from machine to machine across the network. Unlike computer viruses, worms do not require human involvement to propagate. Most worms and viruses are closely related – they both spread and reproduce and their effects can be identical.

Subject Index